FRAUD RISK ASSESSMENT

FRAUD RISK ASSESSMENT
Building a Fraud Audit Program

Leonard W. Vona

WILEY

John Wiley & Sons, Inc.

Library of Congress Cataloging-in-Publication Data

Vona, Leonard W., 1955-
    Fraud risk assessment : building a fraud audit program / Leonard W. Vona.
        p.   cm.
    Includes index.
    ISBN 978-0-470-12945-6 (cloth)
        1. Auditing.   2. Forensic accounting.   3. Fraud—Prevention.   I. Title.
    HF5667.V66 2008
    658.4'73—dc22

2007049354

Contents

Preface   vii

About the Author   ix

Acknowledgments   xi

Chapter 1   Fraud Theory   1

Chapter 2   The Fraud Audit   19

Chapter 3   Organizational Fraud Risk Assessment   37

Chapter 4   Fraud Penetration Risk Assessment   55

Chapter 5   Fraud Data Mining   69

Chapter 6   Fraud in Expenditure   83

Chapter 7   Contract Fraud   107

Chapter 8   Bribery   119

Chapter 9   Travel Expenses   137

Chapter 10   Payroll Fraud Schemes   145

Chapter 11   Revenue Fraud   157

Chapter 12   Asset Fraud Schemes   165

Chapter 13   Fraud Control Theory   169

Chapter 14   Fraud Audit Report   177

Chapter 15   Fraud Investigation for the Auditor   191

Index   203

Preface

People commit fraud. Therefore, corporations, not-for-profit organizations, business systems, personal computers, and cell phones do not. This distinction is simple, but an important one to note. Fraud investigation from the accounting perspective naturally arose from the investigative tenets of auditing. Unfortunately, auditing standards, although requesting that auditors look for fraud, do not provide a way to adapt the existing audit tools to detect fraud. After spending more than thirty years performing diversified auditing and forensic accounting, I have developed a fraud audit theory, the principles of which will assist auditors in what traditionally has been one of their most nebulous responsibilities.

My theory includes the steps of a proactive approach in responding to fraud risk. Using a framework familiar to all auditors, the theory recognizes and categorizes the multitude of fraud schemes. The application of my fraud theory provides the necessary steps needed to, not only detect fraud specific to a situation, but that are indicative of the preventive actions to be taken.

The theory addresses the perpetrator's role in committing the fraudulent act. The auditor is not required to think like a perpetrator of fraud, a useless act, but to be as creative and intuitive in their response to fraud, as the perpetrator is in their pursuit of carrying out a fraudulent act. The difference between right and wrong is simple; however, people complicate the difference, by what they choose to desire. Hopefully, this book will help the profession understand the important consequences of wrongdoing with regards to fraud, thereby, making the auditor better equipped to detect fraud, and, lastly, to confer an understanding of the detrimental consequences of fraud, not only to the individual making the choice to commit fraud, but to society as a whole.

About the Author

Leonard W. Vona is a financial investigator with more than thirty years of diversified auditing and forensic accounting experience, including a distinguished eighteen-year career in private industry. His firm advises clients in the areas of fraud litigation support, financial investigations, and fraud prevention. He has successfully conducted more than one hundred financial investigations. With his extensive trial experience, he is a qualified expert witness and has been cited in West Law for the successful use of circumstantial evidence.

Mr. Vona lectures on fraud topics both nationally and internationally. He regularly speaks at audit conferences, and he has developed the fraud training curriculum for the MIS Training Institute, an internationally recognized audit training organization. Having provided more than one thousand days of fraud training to organizations around the world, he has been a member of the faculties of the National Association of Fraud Examiners and at Rensselaer Polytechnic Institute's Lally School of Management. In addition, Mr. Vona has written the training course on Auditor's Responsibility for Detecting Fraud, SAS No. 99, used by CPA Societies across the nation.

A graduate of Siena College in Loudonville, New York, having received a Bachelor's degree in accounting with honors, Mr. Vona is a Certified Public Accountant and a Certified Fraud Examiner. He was recognized by Arthur Anderson as one of the top 25 Audit Directors in North America. He is a member of the American Institute of Certified Public Accountants, the Association of Certified Fraud Examiners, and the Institute of Internal Auditors. He is a former President of the New York Capital Chapter of the Association of Government Accountants and the founding President of the Albany Chapter of Certified Fraud Examiners.

Acknowledgments

It is interesting to reflect on one's career, and wonder how I could go from Rensselaer Boys Club to writing a book on a subject that has been a part of my life for over thirty years. Undoubtedly, a countless number of professionals have helped me in reaching this point in my career. However, most of the credit goes to the women in my life, who have helped establish the values that have guided me. My perseverance and work ethic, I learned from the example set by my mom, known as Peachy. Compassion, I learned from my grandmother Edith. My choices of right over wrong, I owe to my great-grandmother, Ethel. The shaping of the person I am today is the result of the seemingly endless patience and encouragement given to me by my wife, Pat.

A special thank you needs to be made to Joel Kramer, who provided me with the opportunity to speak about fraud. In addition, I want to thank the MIS Training Institute for providing me with a platform to present my ideas about fraud. I also thank my numerous students over the years, whose questions have helped me improve the articulation of my fraud theory. Lastly, I wish to express my appreciation to my administrative assistant, Melissa Daley, who always kept me organized throughout the writing of this book.

Also, I would like to thank my editor, Shek Cho, for encouraging me to write this book.

Leonard W. Vona

1

Fraud Theory

Auditors today are at a crossroads regarding how to incorporate fraud detection into their audit plans. Sarbanes-Oxley, Public Company Accounting Oversight Board (PCAOB) regulators, and the professional standards of auditing are requiring auditors to give greater consideration to incorporating fraud detection into their audit plan. Companies' boards of directors, management, and the public are asking why is fraud occurring and going undetected in our business systems. Auditors are asking themselves whether fraud can be detected when there is no predication or allegation of a specific fraud.

Traditionally, the auditing profession had two fundamental ways to deal with the fraud question:

1. Search for fraud using a passive approach of testing internal controls. The approach relies on auditors seeing the red flags of fraud. Although few audit programs incorporate specific red flags for audit observation, the assumption is that professional experience will provide auditors with the skills to observe the red flags.

2. React to fraud allegations received through a tip or some other audit source. Since studies continue to indicate that most frauds are detected through tips, we need to ask ourselves how effective past audit approaches have been.

Historically, the profession relied on evaluating the adequacy and effectiveness of internal controls to detect and deter fraud. Auditors would first document the system of internal controls. If internal controls were deemed adequate, the auditors would then test those controls to ensure they were operating as intended by management. The test of internal controls was based on testing a random, unbiased sample of transactions in the business system. Conventionally, audit standards stated that auditors should be alert to the red flags of fraud in the conduct of an audit. Study after study indicates that the lack of professional skepticism is a leading cause for audit failure in detecting fraud.

In one sense, the search for fraud seems like a daunting responsibility. However, fraud in its simplest form should be easy to find. After all, the key to finding fraud is looking where fraud is and has been. This book focuses on the use of fraud auditing to detect fraud in core business systems. Fraud auditing is a proactive audit approach designed to respond to the risk of fraud. Essentially, the fraud audit approach requires auditors to answer these questions:

- Who commits fraud, and how?

- What type of fraud are we looking for?

- Should fraud be viewed as an inherent risk?

- What is the relationship between internal controls and fraud opportunity?

- How is fraud concealed?

- How can we incorporate the fraud theory into our audit approach?

- What are the ways fraud auditing can be used to detect fraud?

BUILDING FRAUD THEORY INTO THE AUDIT PROCESS

Fraud auditing is similar to, but different from traditional auditing in several ways. Typically, an audit starts with an audit plan, whereby, risks are identified through a risk assessment, controls are linked to the risks, sampling plans and audit procedures are developed to address the risk(s) identified. The audit steps are the same regardless of the system(s) being targeted. Throughout the process, the auditor must have an understanding of the system(s) being audited. For example, to audit financial statements, auditors must understand generally accepted accounting principles (GAAP). In the same way, to audit a computer system, auditors must understand information technology (IT) concepts.

Using the Fraud Risk Assessment

If the steps are the same, then what feature makes fraud auditing different from traditional auditing? Simply, the body of knowledge associated with fraud. The fraud theory must be built into the audit process. Specifically, during the audit planning stage, auditors must determine the type and the size of the fraud risk. By performing a fraud risk assessment, the identified fraud risk is associated with the core business systems. As in the traditional audit, controls are linked to the risk, but in this circumstance it is the fraud risk that is targeted. By incorporating the fraud theory in the fraud risk assessment, the concealment strategies employed by the perpetrator(s) are also considered. Auditors rely on the red flags of fraud to prompt awareness of a possible fraudulent event, known as the specific fraud scheme. The sampling plan is used to search for the transaction indicative of the specific fraud scheme. Then, the audit procedure is designed to reveal the true nature of the transaction.

The Principles of Fraud Theory

Although the fraud risk assessment is a practical tool, there are principles upon which fraud auditing is based that auditors should know before initiating a fraud audit plan. These principles are as follows:

- Fraud theory is a body of knowledge.

- Fraud is predictable to the extent of how it will occur in a specific situation, not necessarily in the actual occurrence.

- The key to locating fraud is to look where fraud occurs.

- If you want to recognize fraud, you need to know what fraud looks like.

- People commit fraud, not internal controls.

- Fraud risk and control risk have similarities. However, fraud risk differs from control risk by containing the elements of intent and concealment.

- Fraud audit procedures must be designed to pierce the concealment strategies associated with the fraud scheme.

- Fraud audit procedures must validate the true economic substance of the transaction.

- Fraud audit comments differ from the traditional management letter or internal audit report.

ATM: AWARENESS, THEORY, METHODOLOGY

Fraud is like an ATM machine at a bank. Both are designed to withdraw money. ATM machines enable users to withdraw money from banks. Fraud is the withdrawal of funds from an organization. The funds may be embezzled directly, siphoned off through kickback schemes, or be the result of inflated costs due to bribery and conflict of interests. The fraud audit approach requires awareness, theory, and methodology (ATM) to detect fraud. Successful auditors need:

Awareness of the red flags of fraud:
- Fraud concealment strategies
- Sophistication of the concealment strategy
- Indicators of fraudulent transactions

Theory provides an understanding how fraud occurs in a business environment:
- Fraud definitions
- The fraud triangle

Methodology designed to locate and reveal fraudulent transactions. The methodology employed in designing a fraud audit program consists of the following stages:
- Define the scope of fraud to be included and excluded from the audit program.
- Verify compliance with the applicable professional standards.
- Develop the fraud risk assessment including:
  ○ Identify the type of fraud risk.
  ○ Identify business processes or accounts at risk.
  ○ Internal controls are linked to the fraud risk.
  ○ Concealment strategies revealed using the red flags of fraud.
  ○ Develop a sampling plan to search for the specific fraud scheme.
  ○ Develop the appropriate fraud audit procedures.
- Write the fraud audit report.
- Understand the fraud conversion cycle.
- Perform the fraud investigation.

The search for fraud is built on both awareness and methodology; however, both items are predicated on auditors having a sufficient knowledge of the science of fraud, hence the fraud theory. Auditors are not born understanding fraud. The awareness needs to be incorporated into the audit plan through audit team discussions during the planning stages. Audit programs must incorporate a methodology that responds to the identified fraud risks existing in core business systems.

Theory

The "T" in ATM stands for theory, specifically, fraud theory. Given that the knowledge of fraud theory is needed by auditors in order for "awareness" to be incorporated into the audit plan and for a "methodology" to be established, the specific elements of fraud theory need to be discussed as a first step.

Definitions Inherent to the process of searching for fraud is having a clear definition of fraud to be incorporated into the fraud risk assessment. Throughout the process, a thorough understanding of the fraud theory is critical to an auditor's success in preventing, detecting, deterring, and prosecuting fraud.

Auditors need to understand that fraud is an intentional and deliberate effort by the perpetrator to conceal the true nature of the business transaction. Fraud perpetrators have varying levels of sophistication, opportunity, motives, and skills to commit fraud.

The fraud risk assessment starts with a definition of fraud and the type of fraud facing organizations. The assessment can be based on a legal definition, an accounting definition, or the author's definition specifically designed for fraud risk assessments.

The Legal Definition
- A known misrepresentation of the truth or the concealment of a material fact to induce another to act to their detriment.

- A misrepresentation made recklessly without the belief in its truth to induce another person to act.

- A tort arising from a knowing misrepresentation, concealment of material fact, or reckless misrepresentation made to induce another to act to their detriment.

- Unconscionable dealing especially in contract law. The unfair use of power arising out of the parties' relative positions and resulting in an unconscionable bargain.

The legal definition requires auditors to understand the legal implications of the terms in the definition. The term "misrepresentation" includes concealment, nondisclosure, or false representation. The misrepresentation must relate to a material fact rather than a simple opinion. However, opinions made by an individual purportedly with superior knowledge could become a misrepresentation. Concealment, referred to as suppression of facts, is also a critical aspect of the misrepresentation. The courts have accepted these theories of concealment:

- Intentional concealment of known defects.

- Active prevention of the discovery of the defects.

- Uttering lies, with the intent to deceive.

- Nondisclosure typically does not rise to the level of fraud, unless a fiduciary relationship exists.

In reality, the use of the legal definition of fraud is impractical for most audit organizations simply because the definition is written for civil and criminal prosecutions.

The Accounting Definition   Given the specific usage of the legal definition, auditors typically look to the applicable professional standards followed by the audit organization. The American Institute of Certified Public Accountants (AICPA) offers guidance in its Statement of Auditing Standards (SAS No. 99) as to the auditor's responsibilities to detect fraud that would have a material impact on the financial statements. The standards focus on financial statement and asset misappropriation schemes. Interestingly, the standard does not provide a definition of fraud. Rather auditors are guided by the standard definitions of errors in financial statements. An example of a professional standard applicable to fraud is the Institute of Internal Auditors Standard 1210.A2.

The Institute provides guidance on *Auditor's Responsibilities Relating to Fraud Risk Assessment, Prevention, and Detection.* The standard states that internal auditors should have sufficient knowledge to identify the indicators of fraud, but they are not expected to have the expertise of a person whose primary responsibility is detecting and investigating fraud. The standard contains a section called "What is Fraud." This section states:

Fraud encompasses a range of irregularities and illegal acts characterized by intentional deception or misrepresentation, which an individual knows to be false or does not believe to be true. Throughout this practice advisory, and in PA1210.A.2-2, the guidance may refer to certain actions as "fraud," which may also be legally defined and/or commonly known as corruption. Fraud is perpetrated by a person knowing that it could result in some unauthorized benefit to him or her, to the organization, or to another person, and can be perpetrated by persons outside and inside the organization.

The institute provides guidance on auditor's Practice Advisory 1210. A2-2: *Auditor's Responsibilities Relating to Fraud Investigation, Reporting, Resolution and Communication.*

The Author's Definition of Fraud   Acts committed on the organization or by the organization or for the organization. The acts are committed by an internal or external source and are intentional and concealed. The acts are typically illegal or denote wrongdoing, such as in the cases of: financial misstatement, policy violation, ethical lapse, or a perception issue. The acts cause a loss of company funds, company value, or company reputation, or any unauthorized benefit whether received personally or by others.

The Fraud Triangle   Once a fraud definition has been adopted, the fraud triangle must be incorporated into the fraud audit plan. Therefore, fraud theory includes an understanding the fraud triangle.

The fraud triangle is generally accepted as part of the process of identifying and assessing fraud risk. The concepts are inherently simple. The fraud theory states that for fraud to occur there needs to be rationalization, pressure, and opportunity. The AICPA has referred to these three elements as the fraud risk factors or conditions of fraud.

Rationalization   People rationalize. The reasons vary, but the justification always exists. Fundamentally, rationalization is a conscious decision by the perpetrator to place their needs above the needs of others. The ethical decision process varies by individual, culture, and experience. The ability to identify and rank rationalization is difficult on a person-by-person basis within the audit process, because of the fact that organizations are comprised of a number of individuals. Therefore, at an organizational or departmental level, the issues influencing individuals are easier to determine.

Pressures   The pressures are the events occurring within the organization or in the individual's life. The pressures vary by the global risk factor. With the

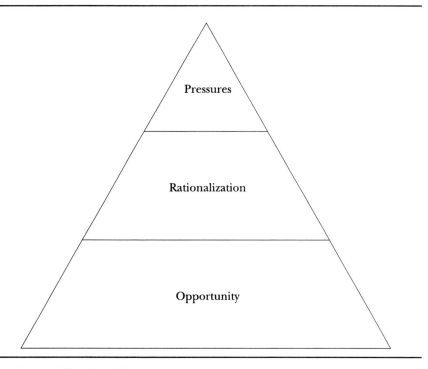

Exhibit 1.1   The Fraud Triangle

pressures of fraud, the individual's personal needs become more important than personal ethics or the organization's needs and goals.

The motive to commit the fraud is often associated with personal pressures and/or corporate pressures on the individual. However, the motive is actually the willful desire to commit the fraudulent act. The motive to commit fraud may be driven by the pressures influencing the individual, by rationalization, or by sheer opportunity.

Opportunity   To commit a fraud, an individual must have access to the asset or manage a control procedure that allows the commission of the fraud scheme. A person's position, as well as, their responsibilities and authorization, also contribute to the opportunity to commit fraud. There is a direct correlation between opportunity to commit fraud and the ability to conceal the fraud. In assessing the fraud risk factor, auditors need to consider both opportunity and the ability to conceal in the design of an audit plan.

Premises   Six premises must be understood in applying the fraud triangle concepts:

1. The three elements of fraud—rationalization, pressure, and opportunity—coexist at different levels per individual.

2. The elements of fraud will vary based on personal circumstances.

3. The strength of one element may cause an individual to commit a fraudulent act.

4. The strength of one element may eliminate the worry of detection.

5. Identifying the three elements is easier than measuring the three elements.

6. The fraud risk factors may originate from internal sources or external sources.

The three elements of fraud coexist at different levels within the organization and influence each individual differently. The strength of one element may cause fraud to occur or some combination of the elements. Perhaps the strength of an element may eliminate the perpetrator's fear of detection. Therefore, the fraud assessment process must consider the fraud conditions.

Measuring the three elements of the fraud triangle is not as simple as taking someone's temperature. The audit process should identify and understand how the fraud conditions lead to the likelihood of fraud. In reality, identifying the fraud condition is easier than measuring the elements. The audit process should be aware of the fraud condition, but ranking the three factors is highly subjective.

Methodology

Methodology addresses the scope of the fraud audit and the subsequent design of the fraud risk assessment. The primary purpose of the fraud risk assessment is to identify the risks of fraud facing an organization. The assessment process evaluates the likelihood of fraud occurring and the extent of exposure to the organization if the fraud event occurs. Such an assessment can be used at various levels of an organization, such as, at the enterprise-wide level or at the business process level. Regardless of level, the assessment methodology must classify the fraud schemes by organizational function. Then a specific fraud scenario can be ascertained for each fraud scheme possible in the organization.

For example, to develop an enterprise-wide fraud risk assessment, the following steps are performed:

1. Create an enterprise-wide category of fraud.

2. Identify the type of fraud that associates with the enterprise-wide category of fraud.

3. Target the major operating units of the organization, for example, company subsidiaries or departments.

4. Target major business systems or accounts in the operating unit, for example, revenue or procurement.

5. Identify the inherent fraud schemes that link to a specific account or business system.

6. Determine the variation of the inherent fraud schemes. This occurs at the business process level.

7. The variation of the fraud scheme is linked to the opportunity to commit the fraud. This is referred to as the fraud scenario.

Fraud Schemes   Through a fraud scheme or "identified fraud risk," a fraud is perpetrated and concealed in a business system such as: account balance, class of transactions, or presentation and disclosure assertions. The fundamental mechanics of fraud schemes are the same for each organization, but how a scheme occurs within each organization may differ. Due to the differences, the identified fraud risks should be considered as an inherent risk. Therefore, in developing the list of fraud schemes for the core business systems, remember these basic tenets:

- Each core business system has a finite list of inherent fraud schemes.

- Each fraud scheme is perpetrated by an individual. This action is referred to as fraud opportunity.

- Each fraud scheme may have a series of variations.
- Each fraud scheme variation has various fraud scenarios.
- Each fraud scheme occurs differently in each industry and each company or organization.
- Each perpetrator is confident that they will not be detected.
- Each fraud scheme has a unique concealment strategy and characteristics.
- Each concealment strategy has associated red flags.
- Each fraud scheme has a unique data profile.
- The objective of each fraud scheme is the initiation of the conversion cycle in which the perpetrator converts the fraud scheme to personal gain.

Inherent Fraud Schemes   The fraud risk assessment process starts with identifying the fundamental fraud scheme, also known as the inherent fraud risk schemes, facing an organization and/or a specific business system. Later chapters will list and describe the inherent fraud schemes.

The Fraud Circle   The fraud circle illustrates the relationship between fraud theory, as discussed in this chapter, with the concept of fraud response and

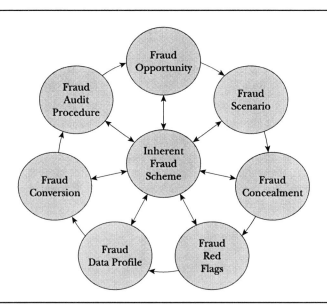

Exhibit 1.2   The Fraud Circle Chart

the fraud audit, as discussed in Chapter 2. Exhibit 1.2 shows how an inherent fraud scheme may be linked to an appropriate fraud response.

Fraud Opportunity Considerations   A person's position in terms of their responsibilities and authority also contribute to the opportunity to commit fraud. The fraud opportunity phase starts with a list of the fraud schemes that individuals can commit by the virtue of their position within the organization. It should be noted that breakdowns in control procedures also create fraud opportunity referred to as internal control inhibitors.

In today's business environment, internal controls do not always function as intended by management. While the business transaction may indicate that the control is functioning, the employee is not performing the control procedure with the control guidelines. The nonperformance of an internal control negates the control's effectiveness. This problem is referred to as the control reality versus control theory.

Fraud occurs because individuals use their positions to intentionally override controls. This override can occur at any level having access to the control, for example, the employee level, the supervisor level, or the senior management level. The override occurs by one person or in collusion with other employees.

In addition, fraud risk assessments should consider logical collusion. Many fraud schemes by their nature can only be committed with such collusion. For example, bribery and corruption schemes occur because of collusion between a vendor or customer, and an employee. Over time, fraud often involves collusion between supervisors and employees. The occurrence of logical collusion does not mean that auditors should consider every possible combination of collusion; nor should auditors ignore the fraud schemes that necessitate collusion.

Fraud may simply occur when no control has been established. This oversight results in management's failure to identify a fraud risk opportunity that allows a fraud scheme to operate undetected.

Understanding the opportunity for fraud to occur allows auditors to identify, which fraud schemes an individual can commit, and how fraud risks occur when the controls do not operate as intended by management. Auditors should also consider the sophistication of the individual committing fraud. One approach to profile individuals is to understand the experience they have in committing the fraud and what motivates them to do so.

Perpetrators of fraud against an organization can be classified into four groups:

1. **First-time offenders.** These individuals have no record of criminal activity. They have either a pressure in their lives that exceeds their income capacity or their rationalized behavior indicates that it is fine to embezzle. Once the pressure or rationalization factor exceeds

the fear of detection, the individuals look for the internal control weakness or the opportunity to commit fraud.

2. **Repeat offenders.** Crime statistics have indicated that people who commit internal fraud have a high tendency to commit the crime more than once. In these instances, the pressure and rationalization aspect of the theory will be less dominant than with the first-time offender. Opportunity becomes the driving force to commit the fraud.

3. **Organized crime groups.** These groups consist of fraud professionals who are external to the organization. The groups may be organized professionally or may be groups of individuals who specialize in a particular type of crime. The key factor is the opportunity to commit the crime. These groups may commit crimes by taking advantage of weak internal controls, bribing or extorting employees, or through collusion with vendors or customers.

4. **Internally committed for the perceived benefit of the corporation.** These crimes are usually committed by employees who believe the act is for the good of the company. Typically, pressures and rationalization for these employees are similar to those of the first-time offender or the repeat offender.

Understanding the individual's crime experience and motivation is a key ingredient to preventing and detecting fraud. The fear of detection is often viewed by management as a deterrent to committing fraud. Once the pressure or rationalization exceeds a certain level, the individual fears the pressure or rationalization more than the fear of detection. The opportunity may also be so persuasive for the perpetrator, that the fear of detection seems remote.

Fraud Scheme Scenario   A fraud risk assessment always begins with the identification of the fundamental fraud scheme, also referred to as the inherent fraud risk. Once identified, the fundamental fraud scheme can be dissected into the variations applicable to the organization and/or its business systems. Once the variation or variations are isolated via control analysis, a fraud scheme scenario can be ascertained. The fraud scheme scenario should describe how the scheme occurs within the organization and/or its business process. The description should identify the opportunity for the fraud to occur and the methods used to conceal the fraud. The scenario could also describe the fraud conversion strategy, in essence, describing how the scheme would occur within the company and the specific business process.

Fraud Variations
Entity and Transaction Variations   Each inherent fraud risk may have several variations. The design of the fraud data mining and/or the fraud audit procedure is dependent on the specific fraud scheme variation.

When analyzing fraud variations, two aspects should be considered: entity variations and transaction variations.

The entity variation analysis identifies how the vendor, customer, or employee would be established or created to provide the appearance of a legitimate source of the fraudulent activity. The transaction analysis identifies variations of how the transaction is processed and recorded due to organizational size, geographic location, management operating style, or nature of the transaction. The variations occur either intentionally or naturally.

The variation analysis should also consider the opportunity to commit the act. At the initial assessment, auditors should identify person responsible for the control procedure and how duties are separated to establish the control environment. The second phase is to consider a logical override or logical collusion by the person responsible for the control procedure.

Industry Variation   Industry fraud variation is defined as the process of converting the inherent fraud risk to a specific risk associated with the industry. By understanding how the fraud risk occurs, auditors can better develop a sampling strategy and a specific audit response for the fraud scheme. How fraud schemes operate in each industry varies by the nature of the industry and the organization. For example, revenue skimming, the diversion of a revenue stream before the transaction is recorded is an inherent fraud risk. Therefore, how the scheme occurs and is concealed in any one industry will vary, but the inherent scheme is still the same.

Awareness

Earlier it was stated that the fraud audit approach requires awareness, theory, and methodology (ATM) to detect fraud. To be successful, auditors need to be especially aware of the red flags of fraud. To comprehend how the red flags of fraud are incorporated into the fraud risk assessment, one must first understand fraud concealment strategies and fraud conversion, both acts performed by the perpetrator(s).

The Red Flags of Fraud   The "red flag of fraud" is a common term associated with fraud identification. The red flag indicates that there is a potential for a fraud scheme. However, it does not necessarily indicate a fraud scenario has occurred. Observing a red flag is the triggering event for a fraud audit. The term red flag is associated with a specific concealment strategy. The perpetrator uses the concealment strategy to hide the fraudulent transaction. The auditor uncovers the fraudulent transaction by observing a red flag event. Red flags can be categorized by control opportunity, fraud data profile or the documentation. Not all red flags have the same weight or value. However, the weight of the red flag or the total number of red flags does correlate with the likelihood of a fraudulent transaction.

Fraud Data Profile   What does a fraudulent transaction look like? In general, the transaction looks like every other one. The fact of the matter is specific data profiles are associated with specific fraud scenarios. When auditors create a fraud data profile, they use data to identify fraudulent transactions within the population of transactions known to a company business system. The data profile will be unique to each specific fraud scheme. In reality, our ability to identity the data profile of a fraud scheme varies by its nature.

Data Mining   Data mining is the process of searching for a transaction that meets the fraud data profile. In essence, when searching for fraud, auditors develop a sampling plan that is focused and biased toward a specific fraud scheme. This sampling, performed as a part of the fraud risk assessment, is referred to as data mining because of the particular transactions being sought.

Fraud Concealment   A key element of the fraud risk assessment concerns concealment strategies employed by the perpetrator(s). The auditors must understand the confidence factor of the perpetrator and concealment strategies associated with the fraud scheme.

The Confidence Factor   Committing a fraud presents the need to conceal the activity. The individual committing the fraud has to have the confidence that the fraud will not be detected. There is a direct correlation between concealment and confidence. If the individual is not confident the act can be concealed, they are not likely to commit the fraud unless the pressures or rationalization factors are so high that the person's logic is overcome.

The Concealment Strategies   When individuals decide to commit internal fraud, a critical aspect of their plan is how to conceal the true nature of the transaction. The goal of perpetrators is to have the business transaction look like a properly approved transaction. Characteristically, each fraud scheme has a method of concealment. However, how individual implements the concealment strategy varies, based on the person's position vis-à-vis opportunity and the company's internal procedures.

The sophistication of the fraud scheme varies with perpetrator. In the simplest strategy, the perpetrator assumes that no one is looking or that the sheer size of the transaction population will hide the fraudulent transaction. An example of a complex strategy would be the use of multiple front companies, which involves management override and off-book bank accounts worldwide.

Methods to conceal the true nature of the transaction will vary with the business system, employee position, the use of computerized systems versus manual systems, required documents, internal controls, and corporate governance issues. In some instances, an individual may use more than one layer of concealment techniques to hide the true nature of the business transaction.

Usually the weak point of the fraud scheme is how the perpetrator conceals the true nature of the transaction. If an auditor can identify the concealment strategy of the fraud and question the transaction, the fraud typically will become apparent. The auditor should also be able to recognize the difference between a generic and a business specific concealment strategy. For example, in the overbilling fraud scheme an inadequate product description is a generic concealment strategy. To identify the related business specific concealment strategy, the auditor must be able to recognize a complete and accurate product description on the vendor's invoice. Generic concealment strategies include:

- Management override. An employee uses their position of authority to approve a transaction or encourage other employees to approve the transaction.

- Collusion. Collusion allows employees to circumvent the control procedures. The employees performing the control procedure provide the illusion that the control is operating. In essence, they provide a false representation of the transaction.

- Blocking the flow of information. This can occur in many ways:
  ○ Layering a transaction. The transaction has to be processed by multiple individuals or entities so no one individual has the full picture.
  ○ Use of intermediaries.
  ○ Labeling the transaction as confidential.
  ○ Using secrecy standards.
  ○ Using people in a position of trust to provide legitimacy.

- Cross-border/geographic distance. Creating a physical distance between the control functions and the location of the documents.

- Direct pressure on manager. The manager is either bribed or extorted to approve a transaction.

- Direct pressure based on the person's relationship with the company. A vendor or a customer causes a company manager to approve a transaction.

- Processing a transaction below the "control radar." The dollar value, nature of the transaction, or management interest is below the control threshold.

- False documentation. False documentation may include an altered, missing, or created document. A professional perpetrator may use advanced techniques that require a forensic document expert to reveal the false document.

- Changes to internal controls or audit trails. These changes diminish the ability to place responsibility for an error.

- Complexity of the transaction. The lack of understanding would diminish the auditor's ability to recognize the concealment strategy.

- Concealing transactions among other transactions. Here the sheer number of transactions enables fraudulent ones to be concealed.

Fraud Conversion

Fraud conversion is the process of converting the fraudulent act to an economic gain for the perpetrator of the act. In essence, it is the money trail. The aim of the fraud audit is to identify a suspicious transaction that warrants an investigation. The investigation gathers evidence that an illegal act has occurred. Depending on the burden of proof required by law, one element of the investigation is to show that the individual received financial gain from the fraudulent act.

Auditors should be aware of the various conversion techniques in order to avoid reaching a false conclusion during the audit process. Typical conversion strategies are:

Theft of Company Funds
- Theft of cash/currency

- Check theft and false endorsement or check alteration

- Counterfeiting of company checks

- Unauthorized charges on company credit cards

- Wire transfers to unauthorized accounts

Embezzlement of company funds:
- Incoming checks negotiated through a look-alike bank account name or false endorsement

- Company check issued to shell company bank account

- Company check issued on other false pretense or disguised purpose

Kickbacks
- Economic gratuities from vendor or customer/goodwill offerings

- Vendor provides goods or services

- Hidden ownership in vendor or customer

- Hiring family or related parties

Asset Conversion
- Sale of company asset
- Theft of asset
- Personal use of an asset without theft
- Use of apartments, boats, or airplanes
- Purchase of asset below fair market value (FMV)

Disguised Third-Party Payments
- Prepaid credit cards and telephone cards
- Gifts
- Event tickets
- Entertainment and travel

Disguised Compensation
- Conflict of interest
- Disguised compensation
- Disguised fringe benefit
- Stock options manipulation
- Undisclosed loans
- Acquisition of asset below FMV
- Misuse of company assets
- Disguised real estate leases

THE FRAUD AUDIT

There are three approaches to a fraud audit: the passive approach, the reactive approach, and the proactive approach. The proactive approach is known herein as the fraud audit approach. Auditors taking this approach are searching for fraud when there is no fraud alleged or there are no control weaknesses indicating fraud occurring. The fraud audit approach can be utilized as an overall response to the risk of fraud. The fraud audit itself is the application of audit procedures to a population of business transactions in a manner to increase the propensity of identifying fraud. These concepts will be discussed in Chapter 2.

Global Risk

Chapter 3 discusses the fraud risk assessment. Specifically, analysis of the purpose of a fraud audit risk assessment from both an enterprise-wide and a business process view.

The Fraud Risk Audit Program

Chapter 4 discusses the fraud risk audit program as it pertains to fraud risk at the mega-risk level. The tool used is the fraud penetration assessment rather than the enterprise-wide risk assessment or the business process risk assessment.

2

The Fraud Audit

Auditing for fraud is not a new concept; it has been embedded in the audit process since its beginning. The question now arises of just how sophisticated the audit process will be in the search for fraud. In its lowest-level sense, the audit process is not designed to search for fraud. If fraud becomes apparent for any reason, the business transaction is investigated. Auditors can detect fraud through the testing of controls and by observing red flags, or the audit process itself may be designed to search for fraud. Three approaches are possible:

1. **Passive approach.** The audit is designed to determine that controls are in place and operating as intended by management. The sampling procedure is random and nonbiased. The audit procedure is intended to determine the existence of controls and to be alert to the red flags of fraud.

2. **Reactive approach.** In the reactive approach, an investigation is performed in response to fraud allegations. In this approach, the procedures are focused on resolving the specific allegation.

3. **Proactive approach or the fraud audit approach.** In this approach, the search for fraud takes place when there is no fraud allegation or internal control weakness that would suggest fraud is occurring.

THE AUDIT RESPONSE

At one time, auditors did not believe it was their job to detect fraud. The professional standards avoided the word "fraud." Prior standards used words like "error," "irregularities," and "omissions." However, professional audit standards are changing, and they now require auditors to respond to the risk of fraud. Statement of Auditing Standards No. 99 issued by the American Institute of Certified Public Accountants (AICPA) requires an auditor to respond to the risk of fraud that could have a material impact to the financial statements. The statement specifically requires audit procedures for management override, revenue misstatement, and other identified fraud risks. Regardless of the required audit procedures, the audit must respond to the risk of fraud. Although the term fraud auditing is new, the auditor's responsibility to search for fraud has not fundamentally changed.

The audit plan starts with an understanding of how assertive, or fraud sophisticated, the plan will be in the pursuit of uncovering fraud. The six typical responses to fraud are:

1. Take no specific audit response to the risk of fraud.

2. Perform a fraud risk assessment and identify the controls that are in place to manage the risk of fraud.

3. Observe the red flags of fraud by testing the internal controls.

4. Perform a fraud audit of the business system or financial accounts.

5. Integrate fraud audit procedures to locate fraudulent transactions in the core business systems.

6. Respond to allegations of fraud via an investigation.

The fundamental audit plan has two basic components: the sampling procedure and the audit procedure. The traditional audit sampling procedure is a random, unbiased approach designed to offer an opinion on the internal controls. The sampling procedure in a fraud audit is a nonrandom, biased approach designed to search for a specific fraud scheme. The fraud sampling procedure can be thought of as what was traditionally called discovery sampling.

Similarly, the other component of the audit plan, the audit procedure, traditionally was designed to test controls. The purpose of testing internal controls is to provide direct evidence that internal controls are in place and operating as intended by management and indirect evidence that fraud has not occurred. However, in terms of the fraud audit plan, audit procedure is designed to detect the fraud scheme. Specifically, fraud auditing is designed to provide direct evidence concerning the existence of a specific fraud scheme and indirect evidence that controls are in place and operating as intended by management. The differences in the traditional audit plan and the fraud audit plan are not an indication of whether one is a good and the other a bad audit plan. The question is how fraud-assertive and fraud-sophisticated the audit plan should be designed.

No Specific Audit Response

The audit plan relies on the auditor observing fraudulent transactions without any specific guidance.

In this passive approach, an organization relies solely on the fraud monitoring procedures to identify transactions that should be investigated. These procedures may include the organization's fraud hot line, awareness by management, or the organizational fraud monitoring internal controls.

Fraud Risk Assessment and Control Identification

The audit plan identifies fraud risks that are inherent to the business operation. The fraud scenarios are developed and correlated to the internal controls. Therefore, the fundamental premise of this response is: if internal controls are adequately designed, then the likelihood of fraud occurring is minimized.

Being a passive approach to searching for fraud, the auditors select a random, nonbiased audit sample or a judgmental audit sample. Then they perform an internal control walk-through to determine if controls are in place and operating as designed by management. If internal controls are operating as intended by management, the audit conclusion is that fraud is not likely because of the adequacy and effectiveness of the internal controls.

Observe the Red Flags of Fraud by Testing Internal Controls

Traditionally, auditing has focused on testing internal controls and examining documents to observe evidence regarding the performance of the internal controls. The audit standards have suggested that auditors be aware of the red flags of fraud without distinguishing a red flag associated with fraud. Therefore, audit plans have not included the fraud-specific red flags that auditors should look for. In essence, the plans relied on the experience of the individual auditors to observe red flags. As a result, the detection of fraud depended on the fraud experience of the individual auditor because the audit plan was not built to respond to the inherent fraud risks.

The method of using red flags specific to a fraudulent activity differs from the previously discussed responses to fraud, and, therefore, it deviates from the traditional use of audit red flags. One way in which the method differs is its use in sample design, where it can be focused either on the fraud being committed or on random transactions. If the approach to sampling were fraud focused, the transaction search would target those transactions consistent with the specific fraud scheme. Therefore, it is considered a reactive approach to searching for fraud.

In addition, the audit planning session should include discussion about specific fraud schemes and the red flags associated with the entity being audited. By doing so, the auditors ascertain the fraud scheme profile. Then the red flags included in the audit plan act as a specific test.

Once a red flag is triggered, the audit plan should have incorporated a corresponding fraud audit procedure to resolve the fraudulent activity. The auditor's response to the red flag is noted in the work paper. As a result, the work paper contains specific evidence concerning whether the fraud red flags occurred and the auditor's response to them.

Auditors should remember that one size does not fit all when developing the red flags of a fraud scheme. Yes, there can be overlap between the fraud schemes, but the process of identifying red flags should be performed for each individual fraud scheme. The type of event and pattern of activity can correlate types of red flags to a fraud scheme. For example, the red flags of a fictitious company or a false billing scheme would differ from the red flags of a bid-rigging scheme. (See Exhibit 2.1)

Types of Events   These types of events will vary by the nature of the fraud scheme or the industry. This list provides some observable events that auditors might note:

- Internal control
  - Control exceptions
  - Missing internal control
  - Change to an internal control that decreases the audit trail or effectiveness of the internal control
  - Override of an internal control
  - Nonperformance of control
- Transactional data
  - Control numbers
  - Account activity
  - Amounts
  - Correlation of various controls
  - Errors
- Document
  - Document files
  - Document condition
  - Data on documents
  - Signature lines
  - Electronic meta data identifying information

- Control access or visibility
  - Changes to audit trail
  - Control flow of information
  - Timing of event
- Economic substance of the transaction
  - Existence of the event
  - Occurrence of the event
- Employee behavior either consistent with control or changes
  - Lifestyle changes
  - Workplace

Types of Patterns   The types of patterns typically are:

- Anomalies, extreme deviations from the norm
- Missing information, lacking pertinent factual data
- Vagueness/specific, either unclear or overly specific
- Unusual or abnormal, irregular or uncommon
- Illogical, contrary to what seems reasonable
- Frequency, consistent and habitual actions
- Ranges, extent or scope of an action
- Trends, actions that tend to progress in the same general direction
- Change, a difference that appears distinctly different
- Error, information is incorrect
- Arithmetic, calculation error

Linking the Event with the Pattern   The audit process must link the observable event with the pattern of activity. Examples of this linking follow.

- Vendor invoice numbers in a sequential order or a limited range would be an indication of a *false billing scheme with a front company.*
- A vendor invoice that lacks an adequate product description would be indicative of an *overbilling scheme or a front company scheme.*
- Purchases from one vendor having an extreme range of commodity codes would indicate a *pass-through front company scheme.*

Exhibit 2.1 Red Flags of Vendor Invoices

Company Name
Matrix Red Flags Theory
Risk Unit: Red Flags of Vendor Invoices

Type of Red Flag	Document Condition and Information	Internal Control Considerations	Transactional Considerations	Processing or Recording	Other
Anomaly	Copies versus originals	Check returned or held for manager	Consistency in pattern of billing (i.e., every week on Monday)	Documentation retained in non–accounts payable file	Executive involved with small dollar
Vagueness	Lack of clear product description and quantity	Several invoices applied to open purchase order	None	Charge in high-volume account	Name of vendor
Restrictive	No vendor telephone or physical address	Vendor used by one manager only	None	Paid same day entered into accounts payable	All questions directed to vice president
Missing	No customer order number; no vendor invoice	No purchase order or receiving report	No ship-to address information	None	None
Illogical	No vendor Web site; Paper type inconsistent/consistent with expectation	Improper approval	Sequential invoice numbers or invoice numbers not in date order	Purchase order date after invoice date	Consistent even amounts

Frequency	Invoice occurrence not consistent with expectation	Vendor invoice amount greater than purchase order	None	Manager inquiries about payment status	Small dollar below control threshold
Range	None	Invoice amounts consistently below control thresholds	Vendor invoice numbers limited or too great	None	Pattern of overspending
Change	Format and style of invoice varies	Address or bank account; Line budget increase for expense.	None	Regular journal transfer of charges	Supplier change correlates to manager or event change
Error	Sales tax or VAT incorrect	Invoice does not match underling records	Control numbers entered into system incorrectly	Recorded to improper account	Duplicate payment
Arithmetic	Charges do not total	No independent check of totals	None	None	Improper calculation of tax or add-on charges
Unusual	No typical add-on charges for industry	Handwritten additional charges	Invoice or purchase order has letters, special symbols not on documents	Handwritten special instructions	Use of small business software to create invoice

Building Fraud Red Flags into the Audit Plan   The building of the fraud red flags into the audit plan requires eight steps:

1. Determine the specific fraud scheme and the fraud scheme variation.

2. Identify the opportunity to commit the fraud scheme, thereby developing the fraud scenarios.

3. Link the concealment strategies to the specific fraud scheme.

4. Identify the red flag through an event that can be observed and measured by the auditor.

5. Link the red flag to the concealment strategy.

6. Identify a red flag triggering event that tells the auditor to perform additional audit procedures.

7. Identify the fraud audit procedure to resolve the red flag.

8. Derive all possible conclusions.

Example of the Red Flag Audit Approach

- An inherent fraud scheme in the procurement process is referred to as *the favored vendor.*

- A fraud variation and concealment strategy in the favored vendor fraud scheme is *bid avoidance using the aggregate purchasing concept.*

- The scheme operates by stating in the request for proposal (RFP) that 1,000 units will be purchased. In fact, however, the real intent is to purchase 10,000 units. The favored vendor receives advance communication of the real intent. This strategy provides the favored vendor with the opportunity to bid at a lower price than the other vendors.

- The red flag is when actual purchases exceed the RFP by a threshold amount. To illustrate, if the actual purchases over a 12-month time exceed the RFP amount by 20 percent, this is a red flag of the occurrence of the fraud scheme. The auditor would then need to perform additional procedures to determine if procurement knew or should have known that the actual purchase would exceed the RFP amount.

- Auditors may arrive at three possible conclusions:

    1. No red flag was observed.

    2. A red flag observed was resolved. Therefore, no apparent fraud exists.

    3. A red flag was observed and not resolved. The red flag was not resolved by additional audit procedures, and the transaction was identified as a suspicious transaction warranting an internal investigation.

Performing a Fraud Audit of the Business System or Financial Accounts

A *fraud audit* is the application of audit procedures to a population of business transactions to increase the likelihood of identifying fraud. Instituting a fraud audit as a response to uncovering fraud is a proactive approach. Consequently, such an approach to searching for fraud can be thought of as the fraud audit approach. The fraud audit approach can be performed as an overall response to the risk of fraud or as a response to an internal control assessment indicating likelihood of fraud or error significance. The goal in performing a fraud audit is to offer an opinion regarding the existence of fraud, and not on the operating effectiveness of internal controls.

The sample selection uses data mining to search for transactions that are consistent with a specific fraud scheme, and correlate to a data profile of a specific variation of the fraud scheme. The sampling procedure is focused on and biased toward a specific fraud scheme. The audit procedures are designed to pierce the concealment strategy by collecting evidence that is independent of the perpetrator of the fraud scheme. The fraud audit consists of 10 steps:

1. Identify the inherent fraud scheme.

2. Identify the various fraud scheme variations.

3. Identify the concealment strategies and the associated red flags.

4. Identify the fraud opportunities.

5. Develop the fraud scenario.

6. Build a data profile of the fraud scheme.

7. Use data-mining techniques to search for the transactions consistent with the data profile.

8. Design the audit procedure.

9. Consider the sufficiency, reliability, and authenticity of the collected evidence.

10. Formulate a fraud conclusion.

The basis of a fraud audit differs from that of a traditional audit in the following ways:

• The fraud audit does not test for the existence of controls.

• The fraud audit does not rely on management representations, nor does it assume falsity of representations.

- The fraud audit affirms the authenticity of the transaction.
- With the fraud audit two conclusions are possible:
  1. There is no known evidence of fraud resulting in indirect evidence that the control is operating.
  2. A suspicious transaction is identified, thereby, providing evidence of fraud.

Inherent Fraud Schemes   The fraud audit approach is designed to search for a specific type of error. In fraud auditing, the error is referred to as a specific identified fraud scheme. Since business systems can include several fraud schemes, auditors must consider which fraud schemes to include in the audit plan. The starting point is the fraud risk assessment.

Example

In the payroll system, a ghost employee is a common fraud scheme that has at least seven different variations. The data mining for each variation differs. Consequently, the audit procedure would pertain to the specific variation. Think for a moment about the difference between a fictitious ghost employee and a no-show ghost employee scheme. The typical audit procedure for ghost employees is to examine personal identification to verify each employee's identity. However, the identity audit procedures for a no-show ghost employee would provide a false conclusion. The no-show employee exists; however, he or she does not provide services for the paycheck. The correct audit procedure for the no-show ghost employee is to gather evidence regarding work performance.

So, it is important to note, that one audit procedure may detect multiple fraud schemes or fraud scheme variations, therefore; auditors should employ audit procedures on a scheme by scheme basis.

The Fraud Scenario   Auditors must answer by whom, where, and how the fraud scheme could occur. The process of finding answers to these questions requires the development of the fraud scenario. Specifically, auditors need to understand the control environment, internal control procedures, inherent business risks, the difference between control theory and control reality, the internal control inhibitors, and fraud concealment strategies by specific fraud scheme.

Fraud Opportunity   People commit fraud. Therefore, an understanding of who could commit the fraud scheme is required. The knowledge of possible perpetrators improves auditors' awareness. The process of identifying the individuals, either internal or external to the company, who have the opportunity to commit or participate in the fraud scheme, is the first step. Owners of an internal control function act like "gatekeepers" by determining what goes through the gate and what is kept out. These owners can keep fraud out or let the fraud through the gate. The steps are:

1. Identify the owners of the key internal controls.

2. Link the control ownership to its inherent fraud scheme.

3. Create an inventory of inherent fraud schemes by control owner.

4. Consider the intuitive factors that may negatively affect the internal controls:

   ○ Fraud risk factors

   ○ Internal control inhibitors

   ○ Differences between physical separation of duties and logical separation of duties

   ○ Differences between internal control theory and internal control reality

5. Identify the logical override of internal control relationships.

6. Determine if all transaction types are processed in the same manner.

The "Understand Factors" How the internal controls function within the organization requires an assessment of the controls that is both analytical and intuitive. The traditional method of identifying control procedures as stated by the organization is an analytical one. The controls are documented and matched to the fraud risks. Then auditors analyze whether the control, as stated, will minimize the fraud risk to an acceptable level. The intuitive aspect of the assessment requires auditors to use professional judgment as to who, where, and how fraud might occur.

The process of identifying individuals who have the opportunity to commit fraud involves the steps listed in the section above. One of these steps states that there are intuitive factors that negatively influence internal controls. These factors are called "understand factors." Discussions regarding them are intended to develop auditors' awareness, thereby, resulting in their improved ability to detect fraud. Specifically, by incorporating these factors into the audit plan, auditors improve their ways of identifying where fraud can occur. The following is a list of the "understand factors":

- The *fraud risk factor* first considers the fraud triangle to assess the fraud opportunity, pressures, and rationalization facing the organization or business unit. Secondary considerations are based on auditors' industry knowledge as to where and how the fraud scheme would occur, industry or company ethical reputation, business geographic location, organizational size, complexity of the business transaction, access to currency, and management operating style. These considerations are often called the *soft controls*.

- *Internal control inhibitors* are environmental factors that reduce the effectiveness of the control. There is evidence of the control procedure occurring, but the control does not function as stated. Nonperformance of control procedures can occur because employees lack time, understanding, and training. Other reasons include: employees are fatigued, failure of the management approval process, lack of organizational commitment to control procedures, and lack of separation of duties.

- *Physical Separation of Duties versus Logical Separation of Duties.* Inherent in the control concept is that one individual does not have excessive control over an activity. For example, in the disbursement cycle, it is typical to separate the vendor master file update capacity from the vendor input and vendor payment function. In the search for fraud, auditors need to understand how the control function actually operates in the business environment.

    To illustrate the concept: If a manager submits a vendor invoice for payment for a new vendor, does the employee responsible for vendor file administration update the vendor master file based on the properly approved vendor invoice, or does the function perform an integrity test to confirm the vendor is a real vendor? If the vendor master file is updated, then the manager has logically updated the master file without ever performing a single keystroke.

- *Control Theory versus Control Reality.* To illustrate the concept of control theory versus control reality, assume these facts. The senior vice president of marketing has eight managers operating around the world. The travel policy allows for reimbursement of actual travel expenses. Each manager travels five days a week. Each travel voucher has a proper approval signature from the senior vice president, which indicates that he has reviewed the expenses and the associated receipts supporting the charge. Further, assume that a proper review of the expenses would require 15 minutes. That would require the vice president to allocate two hours a week simply to approving travel expenses. When looking at control inhibitors, auditors would have to assess whether the vice president is merely signing the expense report or whether he actually examines the supporting receipts. Hence, what really happens with the control differs from the intention.

Logical Collusion   Logical collusion is the assessment of what parties would logically conspire to override the separation of duties and commit a specific fraud scheme. In a bribery or kickback scheme, a manager and vendor would conspire to commit a fraud scheme. In an overtime payment scheme, a manager and employee could conspire to overstate the actual hours worked.

Transaction Type   The auditor should determine if all transactions processed through a system adhere to all key internal controls. When a transaction logically bypasses a key control different fraud opportunities can occur.

To illustrate the concept: Purchases of tangible goods are verified by an independent receiving function. The accounts payable function matches the receiving report to the vendor invoice before payment, whereas, the purchase of services does not always have an independent receiving function. Therefore, service expenditures have a different fraud opportunity in purchase for goods.

Example

The terminated ghost employee scheme starts with a real employee who performs real job duties. The employee terminates employment and the termination is not reported to human resources. The supervisor keeps the employee on the payroll, falsifies time records, and diverts the employee's check.

In the case of a foreign national, the supervisor does not worry about tax reporting requirements. In the case of a surprise payroll test, the supervisor states that the employee has left the country.

Entry-level positions often have employees that simply do not show up for work. Once again, the supervisor falsifies the time record and diverts the paycheck. Departments with entry-level positions where the actual payroll expense does not match to the payroll budget would be an easy place to commit the fraud scheme.

In case of direct deposit, the supervisor would provide a fictitious request for change of bank account information. In a retail environment, the store manager could actually cash the paycheck in the cash register.

Data Profile   The data profile is the process of drawing a picture of the fraudulent transaction using recorded information. Business systems are comprised of tables of information that can be mapped in a way to identify transactions consistent with the fraud theory. Building the data profile is the first step to effective data mining. The second step is the actual data-mining techniques.

Data Mining   The purpose of data mining is to identify a discrete number of transactions that can be examined using fraud procedures. In essence, which transaction has a higher propensity of fraud than other transactions? It differs from the sampling plan performed as a part of a traditional audit because it is focused and biased toward a specific type of error. In this case, the error correlates to the specific identified fraud risk. Chapter 5 discusses the concept of data mining in depth.

Audit Procedure Design   Fraud audit procedures are designed to determine the true nature of the business transaction. The procedure does not test the existence of the internal controls or rely on management representations. Nor does the procedure assume the falsity of the transaction. By design, the procedure focuses on the concealment strategy and associated red flags. Fraud audit procedures are:

- **Document examination.** Documents are examined for the red flags of fraud.

- **Economic substance procedure.** Procedures are performed to determine that the transaction occurred and the asset exits.

- **Independent data comparison.** Procedures are performed to compare the transaction to a database not under the control of the perpetrator. The database may be an electronic file, paper file, or interview.

- **Logic testing.** The transaction is analyzed to determine whether it is consistent with logical business sense.

- **Trend analysis.** Auditors determine whether the transaction pattern of activity is consistent with a predictable pattern of activity.

- **Fraud magnitude test.** Auditors develop an economic model to predict whether the dollar value of the transaction is consistent with a predictable dollar outcome.

Example

The *data-mining stratification* starts with all terminated employees. The data mining could isolate terminated ghost employees who recently changed their address or bank account information or whose information matches that of another employee. Other strategies focus on employees who are foreign nationals, transient, or who work at home because by their nature they are not as visible. Departments with entry-level positions and routine turnover would also fit the profile.

The *audit strategy* focuses on the terminated ghost employee scheme variation. The audit procedure would focus on work performance documents in the weeks near the end of the employment period (i.e., comparing the employee's reported hours to work schedules for the final four weeks the employee is listed on the payroll register). If the employee were not listed on the work schedule, that condition would be a red flag of the fraud scheme. The fraud audit procedures would differ in these ways:

- **Documentary examination.** The handwriting on the last four time cards does not match the employee's handwriting on pre-employment documents.

- **Economic substance procedure.** Confirm with the terminated employee his or her recollection of the termination date.

- **Independent data comparison.** Determine if the building access control register lists the employee. Examine the computer security access log for signs of computer log on entries. (See Exhibit 2.2)

Evidence Consideration Audit procedures, by design, collect evidence that allows auditors to formulate conclusions regarding the transaction. In fraud audits, there is an inherent assumption that the fraudulent transaction will be concealed, documents will be falsified, and internal controls will not function as intended by management. In essence, the perpetrator of the fraud has made false representations regarding the transaction.

The design of the audit procedure should consider the quality of the evidence gathered, availability of evidence related to the fraud scheme, and how auditors would be deceived through the acceptance of the audit evidence. From a legal perspective, the fraud audit procedure should consider the sufficiency, reliability, and authenticity of the evidence consistent with the criminal or civil procedures for admissible evidence.

An evidence matrix can facilitate the process of considering the evidence by focusing on who created the evidence and where the evidence is stored. Logically, evidence obtained from a source independent of the perpetrator is more reliable than documents created and stored under the control of the perpetrator. The goal of fraud auditing is to obtain evidence from a source not under the control of the fraud perpetrator and to understand the red flags of false documents.

The location of the evidence is referred to as the on-the-books or off-the-books analysis. On-the-books records are those located within the organization that is being audited. Off-the-books records are those that are located at a third-party organization. If the fraud scheme is completely an on-the-book scheme, it generally can be resolved by document examination. A fraud scheme involving off-the-book records, however, will require the cooperation of the third party or a confession from the perpetrator.

The design of the audit procedure with regard to evidence is critical, so that auditors know from the beginning of the fraud audit what logical conclusions can be reached regarding the fraud scheme. Otherwise,

Exhibit 2.2 Asset Misappropriation: Ghost Employee

Company Name
Matrix Fraud Theory and Fraud Audit
Risk Unit: Asset Misappropriation: Ghost Employee

Fraud: Type/Scheme	Control Opportunity	Occurs/Fraud Scenario	Concealment	Red Flags	Conversion
Embezzlement/Ghost Employee/Fictitious	Supervisor; Payroll; Human resources	Remote hiring allows supervisor to bypass human resources; Collusion between supervisor and payroll	False ID documents; False time records; No personnel file	Missing documents; Similar handwriting to supervisor; No personal time	False endorsement of check; Set up bank account in name of false employee
Embezzlement/Ghost Employee/Terminated	Supervisor; Employee becomes no-show ghost	Supervisor does not notify human resources of employee termination	False time records; False change to direct deposit	Check endorsement; Change in direct deposit; Change in creating time records	False endorsement of check; Change direct deposit account number
Embezzlement/Ghost Employee/No Show	Supervisor and employee	Collusion between supervisor and no-show employee	False time records	No work space, telephone number, or computer log-on; No personal time	No-show employee negotiates payroll check in personal bank account

Company Name
Matrix Test of Fraud Red Flags
Risk Unit: Asset Misappropriation: Test of Internal Controls

Fraud: Type/Scheme	Sampling Strategy	Data Mining	Test of Controls Audit Procedure	Fraud Audit Procedure	Fraud Conclusion
Embezzlement/Ghost Employee/Fictitious	Data mining	Search on attributes of fictitious employee	See Audit Program Step 7	Physical inspection; Examine original ID documents	Document Fraud; Conclusion
Embezzlement/Ghost Employee/Terminated Ghost	Data mining	Duplicate bank account numbers; Identify terminated employees; Search for changes	See Audit Program Step 7	Compare final time card to personnel file or job schedule.	Document Fraud; Conclusion
Embezzlement/Ghost Employee/No Show	Block sample for a time period or department	None	See Audit Program Step 7	Determine evidence of work performance	Document Fraud; Conclusion

auditors will eventually conclude that they know the fraud scheme occurred, but cannot prove it.

Formulate a Fraud Conclusion   The goal of any audit procedure is the formulation of a conclusion regarding the transaction examined. In the fraud audit, there are two possible conclusions:

1. **There is no evidence that the transaction is fraudulent.** No red flags were identified or the fraud audit procedure did not reveal a suspicious transaction.

2. **Sufficient and credible evidence exist to suggest that an investigation is warranted.** The audit plan should establish when a transaction is suspicious and warrants a fraud investigation.

A suspicious transaction is one, that contains fraud indicators consistent with the fraud data profile, and auditors are unable to make a conclusion regarding the propriety of the transaction. The reasons the auditors designing the audit plan should establish the criteria a suspicious transaction are twofold. The first is to establish a logical end of the audit process. At what point have the auditors gathered sufficient evidence to recommend that the transaction be investigated. The second is to protect attorney work product and privileged communication rights that may exist.

Auditors should understand that evidence gathered as part of the audit process will not have legal privileges, whereas, evidence gathered as part of an investigation under the direction of an attorney may have certain protections. The goal is not to hide information but rather provide a sensible business option. The suspicious transaction would establish a point at which the audit should convert from an audit process to an investigation process.

Integrate Fraud Audit Procedures to Locate Fraudulent Transactions in the Core Business Systems

This response to fraud is also proactive in that it uses the previously discussed fraud audit and builds upon it to develop a fraud audit program. It goes beyond the audit of a business system or financial accounts in searching for fraud by locating fraudulent activity before allegations arise. The manner in which this response integrates the fraud audit and expands upon it will be discussed in Chapter 4.

Respond to Allegations of Fraud Via an Investigation

This response to fraud will be addressed in subsequent chapters, especially, in Chapter 15, in which fraud investigation for the auditor will be covered.

3

Organizational Fraud Risk Assessment

Within the real world, management, consultants, and auditors are preparing and using fraud risk assessment tools to manage fraud risk. An organization's culture is reflected in the risk assessment being utilized in terms of: the level of detail, quantification, and the operating style of management and the auditors. No matter which of these parties prepares the documentation, the fundamental questions are the same. The preparers of the risk assessment documentation need to answer three questions:

1. Are fraud risks identified?

2. Are internal controls linked to the fraud risks?

3. Are fraud risks reduced to an acceptable level?

What differs between the parties is how each use a fraud risk assessment. For example, by using a fraud risk assessment, management is fulfilling its responsibility to manage the risks facing an organization or a business system. The risk assessment document outlines the risk assessment process and it is required as part of the control model. From the auditor's perspective, the fraud risk assessment is the tool that determines the nature, extent, and timing of the audit procedures.

There is no one way to implement a fraud risk assessment. The selection of the methodology depends on the reason for performing the risk assessment. Typically, risk assessments are performed to satisfy regulatory requirements and audit requirements, to gauge internal controls, and to locate fraud in core business systems. In determining the methodology, the question becomes at what level does management and/or the auditors desire to identify and respond to the risk of fraud. Fraud risk assessments can be performed at three levels:

1. **Macro-risk level.** An enterprise-wide risk assessment

    The enterprise-wide fraud risk assessment is designed to provide a comprehensive identification of all fraudulent activities facing an organization and linking the ownership and audit responsibility to the fraud risk. Its purpose is to create a structure for establishing ownership, assessing the likelihood of the fraud occurring, understanding the fraud effect and the methods of how the fraud risk will be managed. The enterprise-wide fraud risk assessment focuses on the internal control environment for determining the likelihood of the fraud risk occurring. The fraud impact should be identified and understood. The organizational culture will determine if a quantitative or descriptive approach will be used to document the fraud impact. Management's objective is to create a structure for managing the cost of fraud.

2. **Micro-risk level.** A business process risk assessment

    The business process fraud risk assessment is designed to identify specific fraud schemes at the business process level, and link specific internal control procedures to the fraud risk inherent to the process. The business-process assessment focuses on internal control procedures, monitoring controls, and those controls associated with information and communication systems. Management's objective is to arrive at the risk mitigation decision. The auditor's objective, while similar, is intended to focus on the development of an audit program.

3. **Mega-risk level.** A fraud penetration risk assessment

    The fraud penetration risk assessment is designed to identify the most likely location of a fraudulent transaction in a specific account, transaction type, and business location. The assessment is used in the development of a fraud audit program that locates and identifies fraudulent activity before allegations of fraud are realized through a hot line, tip, or some unpredictable event. The overall goal of implementing a fraud risk assessment at this level is to locate fraudulent transactions in the core business system.

What is an acceptable level of risk is a question that should be answered before starting the fraud risk assessment. Internal controls provide reasonable, but not absolute assurance of the level of fraud acceptable to an organization. The typical answer is that no fraud is acceptable. While this may be true philosophically, no organization can afford the cost of implementing controls to absolutely prevent fraud.

From a management perspective, the answer will correlate to risk tolerance and the strategies to manage the cost of fraud. Fundamentally, fraud is like any other cost of doing business. The cost should be identified, and controls should be in place to manage the cost at an acceptable level. In this regard, the fraud risk assessment acts as a tool to help management arrive at an informed decision regarding the cost of managing the fraud risk.

All auditors link the organization's risk tolerance to a materiality factor. For example, external auditors issue an opinion on the financial statements to ensure that financial statements are free from material error. Whereas, internal auditors ensure that the internal controls are designed and operated consistent with management's risk tolerance. If the internal auditors do not agree with management's risk tolerance decision, they should report their disagreement to the audit committee.

FRAUD RISK MITIGATION DECISIONS

The importance of a fraud risk assessment as a tool for identifying fraud varies depending upon the perspective of those using it. Management can use the assessment to make considerable decisions, not only about how to handle any uncovered incidents of fraud, but in how to implement stronger controls to prevent future fraud risks. From an auditing perspective, auditors essentially use the fraud risk assessment to address the immediate threat of fraud. Although both management and auditors use the assessment to make important decisions concerning the mitigation of fraud, their perspectives differ given their roles in the process. Regardless of these differing perspectives, the power of the fraud risk assessment becomes evident in its potential uses.

A Management Perspective

Fraud risk assessment occurs at two levels from an organization perspective: the enterprise-wide level and the business process level. At the enterprise-wide level, it is a management tool that identifies where the organization is susceptible to losses that occur from a fraudulent act. The business process fraud risk assessment is designed to identify the fraud schemes that link to the business process or associated type of accounts within the process. Both the fraud risk assessment at the enterprise level and at the business process level can be performed separately, combined, or designed in a manner to mirror each other.

Every organization has an inherent fraud risk. The risk can arise from both internal and external sources, and the fraudulent act can be committed by new employees or long-term employees. The fraud risk factors for an organization include: the nature of the industry, geographic location, organizational structure and size, economic conditions, and management operating style.

Organizations have historically recognized that fraud costs them money. They implement controls to manage known or obvious risks. Risk prevention and security departments address the losses associated with theft or false claims. However, these departments tend to focus on a specific type of fraud. Retail loss prevention departments focus on shoplifting, whereas, such departments in healthcare organizations focus on fraudulent medical claims. Most organizations do not have a systematic approach to identify the entire cost of all types of fraud. Hence, a need exists for an approach to identify all the fraud opportunities facing an organization. The fraud risk assessment is such an approach and, therefore, the starting point for managing the risk of fraud throughout an organization.

An Audit Perspective

The fraud risk assessment enables auditors to concentrate their efforts where the financial statements or the business systems are susceptible to fraudulent acts. Specifically, in performing the fraud risk assessment, auditors focus on the adequacy of internal controls to manage the fraud risk as a basis for determining the nature, extent, and timing of audit procedures. Therefore, the assessment is typically performed at the business process level per existing standards.

The Public Company Accounting Oversight Board (PCAOB) Auditing Standard No. 2 states:

> Fraud considerations in an audit of internal control over financial reporting. The auditor should evaluate all controls specifically intended to address the risks of fraud that have at least a reasonably possible likelihood of having a material effect on the company's financial statements. The controls may be a part of any of the five components of internal control over financial reporting. Controls related to the prevention and detection of fraud often have a pervasive effect on the risk of fraud. Such controls include, but are not limited to, the:
>
> - Controls restraining misappropriation of company assets that could result in a material misstatement of the financial statements;
> - Company's risk assessment processes;
> - Code of ethics/conduct provisions, especially those related to conflicts of interest, related party transactions, illegal acts, and the monitoring of the code by management and the audit committee or board;
> - Adequacy of the internal audit activity and whether the internal audit function reports directly to the audit committee, as well as the extent of the audit committee's involvement and interaction with internal audit; and
> - Adequacy of the company's procedures for handling complaints and for accepting confidential submissions of concerns about questionable accounting or auditing matters.

ENTERPRISE-WIDE RISK ASSESSMENT

The enterprise-wide fraud risk assessment requires the development of a comprehensive organizational overview requiring policy decisions and a complete understanding of the company's business processes. Much like building a house, the strength of the foundation correlates to the strength of the house. The fraud risk assessment is implemented after a thorough base of knowledge is developed. Policy decisions can then be made that are reasonable and effective. In addition, where no one person makes a town, the fraud risk assessment is a collaborative effort of management and the auditor. With this foundation in mind, the steps in developing the enterprise-wide risk assessment are:

1. Develop a methodology to identify and classify the population of fraud risks.

    ○ Include the relevant professional standards.

    ○ Adopt a fraud definition.

    ○ Include the fraud theory: The Fraud Triangle.

2. Perform a fraud likelihood analysis.

    ○ Develop a fraud likelihood score

    ○ Understand and measure the effects of fraud

3. Link the management and audit responsibility to the fraud risk.

Identifying the Population of Fraud Risks

A fraud risk assessment must identify, classify, and measure fraud at entity and business process level. The fraud risk assessment at both the enterprise and business process levels must be linked together to ensure a comprehensive overview. This link is essential for the fraud risk assessment is to identify the major and minor types of fraud risks and link the fraud type to the specific fraud schemes at the business process level. The major types of fraud schemes are:

- Asset misappropriation
- Financial reporting
- Corruption/extortion
- Revenue obtained improperly
- Expense avoidance
- Government regulations avoidance

- Obtaining information outside proper channels or the purposeful loss of information

- Computer fraud

- Management override concerns

The minor types of fraud risk will vary by the major scheme being employed, the organization, and the fraud definition selected for the enterprise-wide risk assessment methodology. The minor types of fraud are both generic to all businesses and specific to the type of business. The expenditure cycle tends to be more generic, whereas, the revenue cycle tends to be more specific to the industry. Exhibit 3.1 illustrates the minor types of fraud associated with the major fraud schemes.

Exhibit 3.1   Enterprise-Wide Risk Structure

Asset Misappropriation, Loss of Funds, or Tangible Assets
- Embezzlement of Funds: The embezzlement includes the theft of currency, disbursements on false pretenses, or the diversion of incoming cash receipts.

- Theft of Tangible Asset: The theft of a tangible asset of the company includes inventory, equipment, and supplies.

- Misuse of Assets: The conversion of a company asset for personal or nonbusiness use.

- Lack of Business Purpose: Expenditure of funds that are not for the benefit of the organization.

- Related Party/Conflict of Interest: Purchases, contracts, or disbursements when an employee has an undisclosed ownership or financial interest in the vendor or the customer.

- Dispose of asset below fair market value (FMV)

- Acquisition of asset above FMV

Misstatement of financial reporting, of the financial statements, or internal financial reporting systems
- Fictitious or sham transactions

- Improper recognition

- Improper measurement: Estimates, calculations, or assumptions

- Improper disclosure or omission

- Misapplication of generally accepted accounting principles (GAAP)

Bribery, Extortion, or Corruption
- Grand corruption
- Petty corruption
- Political corruption
- Internal versus external bribery
- Extortion of vendors or customers
- Purchasing or revenue

Improper Obtaining of Revenue
- Overbilling of customers
- Improper fees or charges
- Deceptive advertising
- Nondisclosure of known defects or hazards
- Market manipulation

Expense Avoidance
- Unfair or illegal labor practices
- Avoidance of guarantee or warrant avoidance
- Misstatement of royalty or contract obligations

Government Regulation Avoidance: The nature of the risk area will depend on the nature of the industry
- Money laundering
- Countries' tax codes
- Prohibited countries
- Privacy legislation
- Government costing regulations

Improper Obtaining or Loss of Information
- Theft or loss of employee, customer, or vendor identify information
- Insider trading information
- Leaking of confidential board of directors meetings
- Trade secrets
- Promotions, sweepstakes, and prizes

Computer Fraud
- Computer hacking
- Security penetration

Exhibit 3.1　Enterprise-Wide Risk Structure *(continued)*

- E-commerce issues
- Program change control

Management Fraud
- Conflict of interest
- Disguised compensation

Other areas
- Environmental
- Employment
- Human rights
- Consumer protection
- Science and technology
- Political oriented

The following examples show how the major type of fraud risk, minor type of fraud risk, major operating unit, and business system are linked through the fraud risk assessment:

Identifying asset misappropriation at the enterprise level
- Major type: Asset misappropriation
- Minor type: Embezzlement of funds
- Major operating unit: ABC Company
- Business system: Disbursements or accounts payable

Identifying a billing fraud scheme at the business process level (step-down process)
- Specific type of account: Professional services
- Fraud scheme: False billing to fictitious vendors
- Fraud scheme variation: False billing to fictitious vendors (The fraud penetration assessment would focus on variations of fictitious vendors and fictitious expenditures.)

Identifying a financial reporting fraud at the enterprise level
- Major type: Financial reporting
- Minor type: Fictitious reported revenue

- Major operating unit: ABC Company

- Business system: Sales reporting system

Identifying a revenue fraud scheme at the business process level (step-down process)
- Specific type of account: Domestic sales

- Fraud scheme: Fictitious revenue to fictitious customers

- Fraud scheme variation: Fictitious revenue to fictitious customers (The fraud penetration assessment would focus on variations of fictitious customers and fictitious revenue.)

Inclusion of the Relevant Professional Standards

Auditors and security professionals identify and assess risk based on professional standards. A certified public accountant (CPA) would look to the generally accepted auditing standards (GAAS); internal auditors would look to the Institute of Internal Auditors (IIA) standards or the Government Auditing Standards. While these are standards, each set differs per source. The risk assessment should state which standards are being used to build the risk assessment.

Adoption of a Fraud Definition

The starting point of the fraud risk assessment is to establish a fraud definition. The American Institute of Certified Public Accountants (AICPA) offers a definition in its auditing standards. The legal profession offers a definition in *Black's Law Dictionary*. The European Parliament offers a definition of fraud within its policies. Countries offer definitions within their laws. By adopting a fraud definition, the risk assessment establishes the scope of the assessment and the associated parameters. The author's definition is:

> **Fraud.** Acts committed on the organization or by the organization or for the organization. The acts are committed by an internal or external source and are intentional and concealed. The acts are typically illegal or denote wrongdoing, such as in the cases of: financial misstatement, policy violation, ethical lapse, or a perception issue. The acts cause a loss of company funds, company value, or company reputation, or any unauthorized benefit whether received personally or by others.

Example

If an organization improperly calculates overtime pay for its employees or misclassifies employees as salaried versus hourly, would this scheme be included in the fraud risk assessment? Interestingly, many auditors would not call this fraud. In reality, the act may be illegal as a violation of the labor law, and, therefore, result in loss of funds due to penalties and adverse publicity for the organization. Still, the illegal act would not necessarily rise to the level of fraud unless management intentionally misclassified the employees and concealed the truth about the classification. Using the traditional fraud definition, the risk would not be included within an organization's fraud risk assessment. However, using the author's definition of fraud, the risk would be addressed under the illegal act provision of the definition and under acts committed by the organization.

Inclusion of the Fraud Theory: The Fraud Triangle   The fraud triangle describes that for fraud to occur, there must be opportunity, pressures, and rationalization. Regarding the enterprise-wide risk assessment, opportunity is associated with the control environment, specifically, the operating unit or owner of the business system. Therefore, auditors should select the specific control procedure. Then, a measurable event should be chosen from that procedure.

Enterprise-Wide Fraud Likelihood Analysis

As the opportunity portion of the fraud triangle is addressed through the analysis of the control environment, the pressures and rationalization portions are included in the fraud likelihood analysis. The fraud risk factors selected for this analysis are based on the type of auditors performing the risk assessment. For example, external auditors would look to the organizational factors. These examples illustrate the concept.

- Board of directors' oversight established through an independent audit committee, meeting the criteria established in the New York Stock Exchange (NYSE) Corporate Governance Rules section 303a.

- Efforts by senior management, such as an ethics hot line is instituted, its function communicated to the employees, and it receives annual promotion.

- An internal audit is implemented using the fraud audit approach as defined in Chapter 2.

- Integrity controls, such as a code of conduct or an ethics policy, are present and promoted annually by senior management.

- Awareness of pressure and rationalization factors, such as negative morale events, changes with internal employee expectations, or new job requirements.

Instead of the organizational factors addressed above, the internal auditors focus on operating units. Examples of such analysis follow:

- Management commitment to antifraud controls, such as implementation of the management fraud risk assessment and self-auditing

- Fraud awareness training on a unit basis performed annually and reinforced with management communication regarding fraud non-tolerance

- Awareness of pressure and rationalization factors, such as unit-level negative morale events and business continuity issues

- History of known fraud issues with regard to the frequency of reported allegations and incidents of known fraud

- Determining the effectiveness in the operation of internal controls based on the results of prior audits and management commitment to the use of internal controls

Developing a Fraud Likelihood Score

The assessing fraud risk should allow for a reasonably consistent technique for measuring the likelihood of fraud. The technique for rating the likelihood of fraud should be agreed to and understood by all members of management. However, agreement with the rating technique and understanding the actual rating are not the same thing. The fraud likelihood rating should result in the assignment of a score. The scoring system can use high, medium, or low or numbers, as long as the rating meets the organization's need for the measurement of the fraud likelihood. By being understood by all parties, the measuring system implemented will result in a meaningful score. A meaningful score should indicate one of the following:

1. The organization exceeds best practices.

2. The organization meets best practices.

3. The organization does not meet best practices.

An example of using a scoring system on an organization's board of directors with regard to audit controls follows:

- Audit committee charter does not contain all the elements of NYSE Corporate Governance Rules section 303a: score of 3

- Audit charter contains the required elements: score of 2

- Audit charter exceeds Rule 303a minimum requirements: score of 1

Understanding and Measuring Fraud Effects

The effects of fraud vary by the nature of the global fraud scheme and the specifically identified fraud risk. It is true of all organizations, if a fraud scheme occurs, then there will be a loss, primarily a monetary one. For example, the type of loss may be a direct loss of funds, loss in market value, indirect costs associated with reacting to the fraudulent act, or a qualitative loss in terms adverse publicity or loss of public confidence. In addition, once a fraudulent act is identified the loss associated with adverse publicity and with the time and effort needed to resolve the issue should be determined as well.

Therefore, auditors need to identify fraud and then understand the fraud impact, in order to place the effects of the fraud into a manageable perspective. Identification and understanding are straightforward steps; measuring the impact is a more difficult and subjective process. The first step is to identify the fraud impact and then calculate the extent of the loss.

Two loss calculations should be considered in determining the extent of the loss: the gross magnitude risk calculation and the net risk loss calculation.

The Gross Magnitude Risk Calculation   In the gross magnitude risk calculation, the maximum loss potential is determined. While organizations seldom suffer the maximum loss, organizations have failed due to fraudulent acts. Enron and Barings Bank are examples of the gross magnitude fraud impact.

Specifically, Barings Bank suffered large losses due to off-the-book stock trades, and, because of the fraudulent acts, the losses exceeded the organization's ability to remain in business. While other financial instituions have suffered losses from fraudulent acts, the acts did not cause them to discontinue, because the discovery of the fraud occurred in time to prevent the growth of the losses to a size that would result in dissolution. In most cases, the loss of a marginal amount, in relation to the size of the organization, would typically result in the loss of the funds, and in adverse publicity, and possibly the termination of a key individual, not closure.

The Net Risk Loss Calculation   The second calculation used in predicting the extent of loss is the net risk loss calculation. This calculation determines the effects of fraud on an organization's internal controls. The net risk loss calculation is the gross magnitude risk calculation adjusted to determine the quality of the perceived antifraud controls. This adjustment results in the calculation of the residual fraud risk, which should be linked to management's risk tolerance level. The scoring system can be numeric or use the PCAOB narrative system. For example, a narrative scoring follows:

- **Inconsequential.** Individually or collectively, an event or events would not prevent achieving a control objective.

- **More than consequential.** Individually or collectively, an event or events would affect control operation, but not considered adverse.

- **Consequential.** Individually or collectively, an event or events would result in an adverse impact on control operation.

Scoring Examples

Consistent with the likelihood of fraud scoring technique, the process of measuring the effects of fraud should include the identification of a risk impact, development of a threshold factor, and assignment of a score. Examples follow:

Asset Loss Due to Internal or External Fraud
- Loss would be less than $100,000.

- Loss would be less than $1 million.

- Loss would exceed $1 million.

Reputation Risk or Adverse Publicity
- Event would have minimal impact on the company's reputation.

- Event would tarnish reputation with effects lasting less than one year.

- Event would tarnish reputation for more than one year.

Impair Conduct of Daily Business
- Event would result in minimal interruption of daily conduct of business.

- Event would affect the organization less than one year.

- Event would affect the organization more than one year.

Adverse Legal Consequence
- Event would result in civil action.

- Event would result in fines or penalties.

- Event would result in class action lawsuits.

Corporate Criminal Action
- Event would result in disbarment from business.

- Event would result in criminal action against operating management.

- Event would result in criminal action against the organization.

Noncompliance with Regulations
- Event would result in no sanctions.

- Event would result in sanctions, no monetary impact.

- Event would result in sanctions with monetary impact.

Linking Management and Audit Responsibilities

The last step in developing a methodology to identify and classify the population of fraud risks is to establish control and audit ownership. The process requires linking every fraud scheme to an owner and auditor. Establishing control ownership enables the responsibility for managing the fraud risk to be assigned to a department. The audit assignment, in terms of internal and external, also assigns responsibility for managing the fraud risk, and such assignment has the benefit of reducing any audit overlap. Two examples of the linking management and audit responsibility to a fraud risk follow:

Financial Reporting Example
- Major type of fraud risk: Financial reporting

- Minor type of fraud risk: Fictitious sales

- Major operating unit: ABC Company

- Account or business system: Sales reporting system

- Specific account: Domestic sales

- Control ownership: Sales department

- Audit ownership: External auditor

Asset Misappropriation Example
- Major type of fraud risk: Asset misappropriation

- Minor type of fraud risk: Embezzlement of funds

- Operating unit: ABC Company

- Account or business system: Disbursements or accounts payable

- Specific account: Professional services

- Control ownership: Finance department

- Audit ownership: Internal audit and external audit

BUSINESS PROCESS FRAUD RISK ASSESSMENT

The enterprise-wide risk assessment provides the framework for the comprehensive fraud risk assessment. Therefore, in global risk terms, the business process model must connect to the enterprise-wide model.

The business process fraud risk assessment identifies the key internal control procedures associated with the various fraud risks inherent to a business process. Once the key internal control procedures are identified, the likelihood of fraud and the extent of the fraud exposure facing the organization must be determined. Chapters 6 through 12 discuss the most common fraud schemes in key business systems. You will need to adapt the inherent risk to your respective industry and organization.

In determining the likelihood of fraud and the extent of the fraud exposure, a fraud matrix is a useful tool for linking internal control procedures to specific fraud risks or for building an audit program that connects the specific fraud audit procedures to specific fraud schemes. Essentially, the matrix begins by linking an internal control procedure to a fraud scheme and ends by offering conclusions on mitigating the fraud risk posed by the specific scheme.

Internal Controls

In general terms, a fraud control strategy focuses on fraud prevention and detection. The process starts with the internal control model applicable in the auditor's country of origin and identifies the relevant control strategies. In the United States, the control model is COSO (Committee of Sponsoring Organizations) enterprise risk management (ERM). Other parts of the world may use a different control model. Within the business process fraud risk assessment, the internal control procedures are identified and matched to the fraud risk. Managing the fraud risk associated with the internal control procedures are discussed in Chapter 13.

Fraud Scheme Identification

Each business system has a limited number of inherent fraud schemes and a finite number of variations of those schemes. The business process risk assessment should first focus on the inherent fraud risks. All the fraud variations could be considered in the fraud penetration risk assessment. The problem with including all the variations in the business fraud risk assessment is that the assessment will become too large to be a useful tool for management. Therefore, the most applicable variations must be identified by the auditors to develop a comprehensive data-mining plan and develop specific audit procedures.

Fraud Opportunity

Who would perpetrate and conceal the fraud scheme in the business systems and what methods they would use is a question relating to the fraud triangle, specifically, the fraud opportunity. The answer will consist of a specific person or a group of people. "Employees who perform invoice approval" is an example of a group of people performing a control procedure. The opportunity to commit the scheme will depend on the number of control opportunities in the business process and the number of people performing the control procedure.

In determining fraud opportunity, auditors must interview management and read policy and procedure manuals. The interviews are intended to confirm that a prevalent understanding of the control procedures exists and to identify business practices that are not described in the policies and procedures. For example, the interview process should assist the auditors' awareness of the override features built into data systems.

Fraud Scenario

The result of identifying the control and linking it to the inherent fraud scheme and the fraud opportunity, determines the fraud scenario. Development of a fraud scenario is necessary to exposing the fraud and instituting appropriate measures to prevent the act from happening again within a specific business process. Therefore, once the fraud scenario is identified, the next step is to understand how the fraud is concealed.

Fraud Concealment

Auditors must understand the concealment techniques used to hide the fraud scheme in order to determine how a control procedure is circumvented. Without analyzing the concealment strategies in terms of existing policy and procedures, the effectiveness of internal controls cannot be properly evaluated.

Formulation of a Conclusion

A conclusion should be formulated addressing whether the internal controls effectively reduced the probability of the fraud risk from occurring. The ranking system employed should be consistent with the ranking system used in the enterprise-wide assessment. As with the enterprise-wide assessment focus is on the likelihood of fraud. Specific to the business process assessment, the likelihood of fraud analysis determines whether the identified controls would prevent the fraud risk from occurring or the probability of the event occurring. In addition, if the fraud risk did occur, would the internal control detect the error in a timely basis? For example, a bank reconciliation is performed within 30 days. By quantifying the number of days under best practice procedures, an error would be detected within a reasonable period of time.

The resulting loss exposure, if the fraud risk does occur, focuses on understanding the maximum risk exposure possible given the specific risk. The loss exposure will vary dependent on the global fraud scheme evident. For example, in an asset misappropriation scheme, a manager deliberately bills a false vendor; the maximum exposure is limited to the manager's departmental budget authority. The key to effective loss exposure analysis is to indicate the actual loss potential. Documentation of the levels of loss exposure necessitates management to comprehend their risk tolerance.

From an audit perspective, the audit program should focus on the fraud risks identified in the business process risk assessment. Consequently, the auditors' risk tolerance is tied to the auditor's level of materiality.

Fraud Conversion

The term "fraud conversion" means how the individual obtains the financial gain. The business process risk assessment does not require identification of the fraud conversion cycle. However, understanding how the scheme converts from an event to financial gain may be helpful in convincing management of the feasibility of the event being real versus purely theoretical. Often people reject inherent schemes because they do not understand or believe the conversion feasibility.

4

Fraud Penetration Risk Assessment

Auditing standards require auditors to assess the likelihood, significance, and pervasiveness of identified fraud risks. While differences exist among the various standards, the intent of all the standards is the same, specifically, to expect auditors to address fraud risk in terms of the nature, timing, and extent of audit procedures. The following discussion provides an explanation of how auditors may develop audit procedures that address fraudulent transactions in the core business system. This step is part of a fraud risk audit program that locates and identifies fraudulent activity before any allegations are realized.

FRAUD RISK AT THE MEGA-RISK LEVEL

Within the fraud audit process, the fraud risk assessment allows the auditors to determine whether internal controls minimize the fraud risk to an acceptable level concerning the financial statements, business systems, or specific accounts. If the assessment results show that a fraud risk could occur and have a significant impact, the auditors should develop an audit procedure that responds to the specifically identified fraud risk as a part of the overall fraud audit program.

Traditional audit risk assessments and fraud audit risk assessments differ in one important aspect. Fraud risk is an intentional, deliberate effort to conceal the truth. The documents are false, the performance of internal controls is misrepresented, and people tell lies. The fraud is concealed within a business system. Therefore, a fraud risk assessment is used to identify concealment strategies associated with the fraud scheme being employed. A type of fraud risk assessment, referred to herein as the fraud penetration assessment, is integral to understanding fraud risk at a mega-risk level.

The Fraud Penetration Assessment

The fraud penetration assessment is designed to search for fraud at the mega-risk level in order to identify control weaknesses that are not evident at the business process level discussed in Chapter 3. By operating at such a level, the assessment design needs to recognize that control opportunity creates fraud opportunity. Fraud by its very nature is concealed and can occur in various ways. A fundamental tenet of the fraud penetration assessment is that fraud is predictable. It is not a question of predicting whether fraud will occur, but how fraud typically occurs in a specific situation. The starting point, as with any fraud risk assessment, is to identify the fundamental fraud scheme, also referred to as the inherent fraud risk.

The Drill-Down Factor   The fraud penetration assessment is intended to "drill down" to the layers at which fraud risk can occur in order to understand how a fraud scheme exists and is concealed by the perpetrator. The objective of this assessment is to identify transactions that have a greater probability of being fraudulent. The process requires both an analytical approach and auditors' intuitive abilities in observing the types and the patterns of red flags associated with a specific fraud scheme.

The fraud penetration assessment includes analysis of transaction type, of the general ledger account, the variations of the specific fraud scheme, and the opportunity created by internal control ownership. The control access opportunity is eventually linked to the appropriate fraud scenario as a part of this type of assessment. This step is important for the auditors' awareness of the inherent conditions that caused the control failure.

The audit process must be designed to address the specific fraud scenario identified. Therefore, the sampling plan is structured to identify or isolate transactions that fit the fraud data profile, and the implemented audit procedure is intended to pierce the specific fraud concealment strategy.

The Fraud Penetration Assessment Steps   The steps of the fraud penetration assessment are similar to the fraud risk assessments discussed in the previous chapters. The first step is to identify the fundamental fraud scheme, also referred to as the inherent fraud risk. With the scheme in mind, the systems (as in the enterprise-wide assessment) or the accounts (as in the business process assessment) at particular risk are identified through their logical association to the identified fraud risk. In the fraud penetration assessment, a global risk is identified, as is the associated type of fraud. For example, if the fundamental fraud scheme is an embezzlement scheme, then the global risk could be asset misappropriation with the type of fraud being the embezzlement of funds (see example on page 65). Then the major operating unit and the account or business system at risk are targeted.

With the generic fraud risk assessment, concealment strategies are realized with the red flags of fraud, and a specific fraud scheme and variation are identified and a fraud scenario is created. At this point, the fraud penetration assessment deviates from the other assessments. Specifically, the fraud penetration assessment incorporates the drill down analysis, the fraud sophistication analysis, the fraud magnitude analysis, and the transactions analysis. The result of these analyses is to link the developed fraud scenarios to appropriate audit response procedures.

Analysis of Transaction Types

Transaction-type analysis is a technique used to stratify the transaction population into a smaller homogeneous group. The goal is to break down the total population into smaller groups of like data in order to identify anomalies within the segregated population. The transaction types are developed through internal control considerations, methods of processing, and business locations. The types are not good or bad, they are just different. The analysis recognizes that different transaction types have different fraud opportunity. By focusing on a specific transaction type, data anomalies or control weaknesses specific to that transaction type become more apparent.

To illustrate the concept of stratifying the population of transactions into smaller logical groupings of like data, consider these possibilities:

- Journal entries could be grouped by source journal postings, adjusting entries, reclassification, consolidating entries, reversal, or top-sided entries. The resulting groups could be made into sub-groups, such as entries after year-end versus during the reporting period, by the individual or location recording the entry, or by the accounts adjusted.

- When grouping refunds, customer refunds may differ between refunds to individuals versus businesses. In evaluating customer refunds, payments to individuals versus businesses may differ as to frequency, dollar range, and reason for refund. Careful analysis may reveal smaller subsets within each group.

Business systems are designed to ensure that a transaction is processed from origination to the final recording in the general ledger. Internal controls are built into the system to minimize both unintentional errors and intentional errors. However, in reality, not all transactions in a given system adhere to all the internal controls in the same manner. For some transactions, the internal control exception is by design; in other instances, the control difference is caused by the control environment. Procedure manuals may not indicate that the transactions are handled differently, but often the controls are applied differently. Therefore, the goal of the assessment is to identify those transactions that may be more prone to fraud because of an inherent control weakness.

The method of processing these transactions varies with the business system responsible for performing the processing. For example, in the disbursement cycle, expenses can be paid with cash, credit card, check, or wire transfer. The payment may require a purchase order, an open purchase order, no purchase order, or a check request. The expenditure may be supported by a receiving report or no receiving report. These factors create different fraud opportunities.

In addition, the business location correlates to: the internal controls in place, the type and dollar range of transactions for the location, the transactions within and outside of the location proximity, and the person performing the function.

General Ledger Account Considerations

The nature and level of transaction activity in a general ledger account correlates to the probability of how a fraud will occur and be concealed within a specific account. The following examples show how a fraud scheme correlates to an account or a series of accounts:

- False billing disbursement schemes often occur in service categories because the invoice is approved by the individual receiving the services.

- Product substitutions often occur in accounts where an item is consumed in the ordinary course of business and, therefore, an ordinary person would not be able to distinguish between the correct product and the substituted product.

- Short shipment occurs in supplies that are not inventoried and consumed in day-to-day operations.

- Cost of sales account tends to have large numbers of transactions. The sheer size of the population provides a concealment strategy.

Fraud Variation

Fraud schemes must be identified within the fraud penetration assessment. To recognize the variation of the fraud scheme being employed, an analysis of variations is performed involving both the entity and transaction. Such analysis includes all the entity combinations for employee, customer, and vendor. The analysis, with regard to entities, is done to understand how entities may be disguised as new entities, changed entities, activated dormant entities, false entities, or embedded entities. Similarly, the analyzing variation, as it pertains to a transaction, involves how the organizational size, geographic location, management operating style, or the nature of the transaction will be used to process a fraudulent transaction. To illustrate how the fraud variation analysis is performed pertaining to fraud in the disbursement cycle, two lists are presented below. The first list of variations pertains to entity variations and the second list pertains to transaction variations.

Entity Fraud Scheme Variations:
- The company does not exist.

- The company was legally created but does not function like one.

- It is a legally created and operating company, but with a false address or bank information.

- It is a legally created company, but dormant as to doing business, with changed address or bank information.

- The name of the fictitious company that uses a similar name to a real company.

- The name of the fictitious company using the name of a real company that has multiple billing addresses.

- Temporary vendors/limited use.

Transactional Fraud Scheme Variations:
- Fictitious companies purchasing fictitious goods or services

- Real companies purchasing fictitious goods or services

- Intentional overbilling
  - Vendor retains the overcharge
  - Vendor kicks back a portion of overcharge

- Schemes involving intentional diversion of purchase rebate or refunds

Fraud Opportunity

Simply stated, people commit fraud. The fraud penetration assessment should include analysis of fraud opportunity. The primary reason for doing so is to ensure that audit procedures are designed to anticipate all fraud combinations and provide maximum auditor awareness.

Exactly how each employee would commit a fraud scheme varies by employee job duties, rank, and a willingness to conspire with others. Fraud concealment strategies can be developed by one, two, or several individuals, while, the individuals committing the fraud are either internal or external to the organization.

The opportunity to commit fraud requires auditors to develop an inventory of fraud schemes that individuals can logically commit by virtue of their job duties. Therefore, the fraud risks should be viewed as inherent risks to a business system. Auditors must become aware of the fraud opportunity for an individual or associated with a job title before the internal control is identified.

Internal Control Ownership

The responsibility for an internal control provides the opportunity to commit and conceal a fraudulent activity. Fundamental fraud theory recognizes that opportunity is an integral part of the fraud triangle. Therefore, the predictability of fraud directly links to the control ownership.

Access to a control function is an integral aspect of committing a fraud scheme. The access can be associated directly with managing the control function, through inherent weaknesses associated with some other aspect of the business process, or through other related duties that are not directly associated with the business process.

The owner of the internal control generally functions like a gatekeeper. The job of the gatekeeper is to decide who goes through the gate and who is prohibited from entering it. Each business system has its own ultimate gatekeeper. While controls can eventually detect fraud perpetrated by the gatekeeper, stopping the gatekeeper from committing fraud is very difficult.

Auditors must recognize the inherent limitations of internal controls to prevent fraud. Essentially, the limitations involve three different types of access: direct, indirect, and other. The following three examples indicate the importance of understanding how internal controls can be circumvented to commit fraud.

Direct Access   The receiving clerk in the warehouse has the opportunity to commit and conceal a fraud scheme. For example, the clerk could commit a theft scheme by concealing the fraud through falsely certifying the receiving report. In addition, the clerk could falsely certify receipt of a product as to quantity or quality, and, then accept a kickback from the vendor. In both circumstances, the clerk has direct access to the internal controls, namely, the receiving report and the receipt certification.

Indirect Access   Accounts payable general control standards suggest that vendor administration, such as updating and changing the vendor master file, should be separated from the invoice approval and invoice payment process within accounts payable function. The physical separation of duties makes inherent sense to all auditors. However, when the following facts apply, a question arises as to the adequacy of the internal controls in place:

- A manager submits a vendor invoice to accounts payable for payment, and the vendor is not on the master file.
- The manager has authority to approve invoices up to $25,000 based on their signature alone.
- The accounts payable function is responsible for ensuring that all disbursements are supported by proper documentation and properly approved.
- Vendor administration duties are separated from vendor invoice processing duties.

The question arises as to what level of control does accounts payable exercise over new vendors. When accounts payable administration sets up the new vendor without validating that the vendor actually exists, a manager can set up a new vendor on their own. While they do not have physical access, they have effective access. From a fraud opportunity perspective, the likelihood of a fictitious vendor on the master file has increased because of the inherent limitations of the control function.

Other Access   A customer service representative typically has access to customer receivable balances and customer activity. In the daily conduct of duties, the representative observes customer credit balances that are over 60 days old. The representative can either submit a fraudulent letter from the customer requesting an address change, or submit an address change on behalf of the customer through the representative's access duties. Then the representative requests for a refund of a credit balance. In processing the customer refund request, accounting observes a credit balance and submits a check request to accounts payable for a customer refund. A check is mailed to the address of record. Thus, the customer service representative has embezzled a customer refund while having no access to accounts payable.

Documents and Signatures

Auditors rely on the examination of documents and evidence of approvals on the documents to establish that internal controls are operating. However, in most fraud schemes, the documents and approvals are false.

Fraud Concealment Strategies Involving Documents   Being aware of the concealment strategies utilizing false documentation is useful to auditors by adding to their ability to detect fraud. Note, however, that auditors are not expected to be document experts. Some examples of concealment strategies and their use of fraudulent documents follow:

- **Missing, destruction of, or no created documents.** The document was required to process the transaction. After processing the transaction, the document is destroyed to eliminate the evidence. If the transaction is found, perpetrators will argue that they processed the transaction according to what the document indicated.

- **Alteration of documents.** This strategy involves changing of a document to hide the original information. Perpetrators may use sophisticated techniques, which include:

  ○ Using a chemical to dissolve the original ink.

  ○ Cut-and-paste techniques that are concealed by providing only a photocopy of the original document.

  ○ Obliteration techniques by writing over the original information on the document.

  ○ Scanning documents into computers and changing them electronically. The altered document is then printed giving the illusion that the document is an original.

- **Creation of documents.** This scheme involves reproducing or copying a document. The creation or counterfeiting of documents has been made easy by desktop publishing. Perpetrators may also gain access to original letterhead and create what appears to be a true and original document. Small business accounting software packages assist in preparing documents that are original in nature but false in reality. Consider these examples of how false documents were used to conceal a fraud.

  ○ A company sales system was not integrated into the general ledger. Each month the sales report would be printed from the sales system. To record the sales in the general ledger, the controller would post the monthly sales total via the total page on the monthly sales report. In order to inflate the monthly sales totals in the general ledger, the controller created his own total page with an inflated sales total.

  ○ A company's chief financial officer scanned the company bank statements into his computer. He then added deposit transactions to the bank statements and reprinted the statements. When the auditor examined the bank statements, all of the reconciling items were listed.

Fraud Concealment Strategies for Approvals   Approval signature is a key control in all business processes. Auditors should be aware of these techniques to forge an approval:

- No attempt is made to resemble genuine signature. The perpetrator relies on the fact that no one knows what the genuine signature looks like.

- The original signature can be traced from an original document.

- A perpetrator can use freehand forgery that closely resembles the genuine signature.

- A genuine signature can be obtained via trickery.

- A genuine signature can deliberately be written illegibly or in disguised manner. In this way, if the fraud is detected, the perpetrators argue that they did not sign the document.

- A genuine signature can be altered after the fact with chemicals.

Although auditors are not expected to be handwriting experts, understanding a few simple signs of forgery is useful to increase auditor awareness:

- Frequency of change on the grasp of the pen or pencil

- Blunt line endings and beginnings

- Poor line quality with wavering and tremor of the line

- Retracing and patching

- Stops in places where writing should be free

BUILDING THE FRAUD AUDIT PROGRAM AT THE MEGA-RISK LEVEL

At the mega-risk level, the fraud audit program requires auditors to consider the fraud sophistication factor, the fraud magnitude analysis, the internal control inhibitors, and the transaction considerations.

The Fraud Sophistication Factor

Every fraudulent transaction has an element of concealment. In some cases, the concealment strategy is simple: No one is looking. However, concealment strategies are often complex and not easily detectable through an audit process. Therefore, to reveal fraud, auditors need to understand how sophisticated concealment strategies can be. Through such understanding, they can design the audit plan to locate the fraudulent transaction and pierce the concealment strategy. Fraud red flags can be incorporated into the audit plan to achieve this objective, as long as, the auditors are aware of the level of sophistication that the perpetrators are operating at. Exhibit 4.1 illustrates the correlation between the sophistication of the fraud concealment strategy and audit detection.

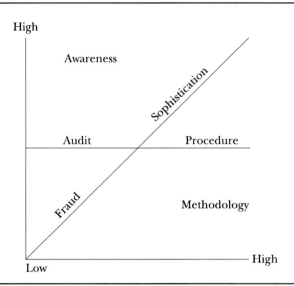

Exhibit 4.1   Fraud Sophistication Chart

Exhibit 4.1 shows that fraud is revealed when the audit procedure is as sophisticated as the concealment strategy. If the procedure is not operating at an equivalent level, the fraud goes undetected. The Exhibit shows that both auditor awareness and audit procedure are directly proportional to the fraud concealment sophistication.

Fraud Magnitude Analysis

Fraud occurs at all dollar levels. A fraud loss may be made up of one $1 million transaction or a million $1 transactions. An old concealment strategy to avoid detection is to keep the dollar value below the control or audit radar. In such schemes, the dollar value of the fraudulent transaction becomes part of the concealment strategy.

Large-dollar transactions may be concealed through a management override feature, whereas small-dollar transactions may be concealed due to less scrutiny of the transactions. For example, procurement card expenditures are indicative of small-dollar transactions that taken together can become more significant.

Control Inhibitors

The fraud penetration assessment is performed in recognition that internal controls do not always operate as intended by management or that the control can appear to be functioning, when in fact it has failed. The typical reasons for control failure associated with fraud are:

- **Collusion.** Collusion allows fraud to occur and go undetected. For fraud, the focus is on logical collusion, not every conceivable collusive opportunity. For example, in a bribery fraud, an employee and vendor collude to commit the fraudulent act. That is a logical combination to consider in the assessing how and where bribery would occur within the company.

- **Management overrides.** Overrides by management provide the illusion that an internal control is functioning when in fact the control failed to prevent or detect the fraud.

- **System override features.** Computer systems have built-in override features to process nonstandard business transactions. These features can also be used to circumvent the intended controls.

- **Nonperformance of control procedures.** Nonperformance occurs when an employee does not perform the control procedure with the vigor intended by the intent or design of the internal control procedure.

- **Nonperforming separation of duties.** Businesses with limited staffing often fail to separate duties, thereby, setting up conditions for collusion, management overrides, and nonperformance of control procedures.

Fraud Penetration Analysis

Background   In this case, the company has a large base of employees who are paid on an hourly basis. The employees are in manufacturing, distribution, call centers, and administrative offices. The company payroll is weekly. Employees receive four weeks' mandatory vacation. Time cards are based on a time clock in the work area.

The Fraud Penetration Assessment Assumptions:
- Fundamental fraud scheme: Time reporting, overpayment of overtime (e.g., an embezzlement scheme)
- Global Risk: Asset misappropriation
- Type of Fraud: Embezzlement of funds
- Major operating unit: ABC Company
- Account or business system: Payroll
- Fraud scheme: Overpayment of over time
- Specific identified fraud risk: Four fraud scenarios could occur and are discussed below.

Audit Program Considerations

Level of Fraud Sophistication: Assume that the fraud perpetrator is a first time offender with minimal sophistication at concealing fraud.

Fraud Magnitude Analysis: Assume that the fraud magnitude analysis is total overtime expenditures. The net fraud magnitude analysis, based on management interviews, would not exceed 3 percent of total overtime expenditures.

Transaction Assumptions: Using the above-listed assumptions, the auditors would focus on those departments in which the identified fraud schemes would be more likely to occur. Then they would question whether there are any employees who do not use the time clock, that have a flexible work schedule, or does the supervisor's span of control or other duties minimize ability to monitor employee activity. The purpose of this questioning is that departments having large overtime budgets and special projects require extensive overtime in a high-pressure situation that creates an environment for fraud to occur.

Data mining considerations would focus on those employees receiving overtime and the pattern to be observed would be on frequency and consistency of overtime use. A high incidence of overtime use by these employees might indicate favoritism or conspiracy. An example of implementing these data mining considerations follows:

Search for Employees
- Receiving 48 or more weeks of overtime
- Whose overtime hours each week are within a 10 percent deviation
- Whose overtime average exceeds a set number of hours
- Who receive the same number of hours a week

Search for Departments
- Where a supervisor must oversee more than 20 employees
- With known past problems
- In which a small group of employees consistently receive overtime

Fraud Scenario and Fraud Audit Procedure

Given all of the above-listed assumptions, the following fraud scenarios would occur in the business environment. The corresponding fraud concealment strategies and audit procedure responses are indicated as well:

1. **Employee overstating hours worked.** The conversion cycle occurs by the employee wages being overstated.

   ○ **Fraud concealment.** The time card is altered after supervisor approval. The employee knows the supervisor does not closely review reported hours or knows the supervisor is unaware of employee arrival and departure times.

   ○ **Audit procedure response.** Inspect time cards for signs of alteration. Compare the time reported to other business systems that capture time events, such as computer security access logs, entry access logs, telephone records, and machine meters.

2. **Employees conspire to trick supervisor on hours worked.** The conversion cycle occurs by the employees' wages being overstated.

   ○ **Fraud concealment.** Employees punch time cards for other employees. Fraud is concealed because the supervisor is unaware of the employee conspiracy.

   ○ **Audit procedure response.** Compare time reported to other business systems that capture time events, such as computer security access logs, entry access logs, telephone records, and machine meters.

3. **Employee and supervisor conspire to overstate hours the employee worked.** The conversion cycle occurs by the employee paying the supervisor a portion of the fraudulent overtime (a kickback).

   ○ **Fraud concealment.** The fraud is concealed via a false approval.

   ○ **Audit procedure response.** The audit response would be the same as for item two. In addition, auditors should identify possible collusive relationships by interviewing coworkers not receiving overtime.

4. **Employee and payroll enter overstated hours.** The conversion cycle occurs by the employee providing the payroll clerk with a kickback based on the overpayment of wages.

   ○ **Fraud concealment.** The payroll clerk alters the time card to support increased hours, falsely approves a change to the card, or creates a new time card and forges the supervisor's signature.

   ○ **Audit procedure response.** Inspect time cards for signs of alteration and forgeries. Confirm hours paid through interviews of supervisors.

5. **Payroll employees falsely overstate their own hours worked.** The conversion cycle occurs by payroll employees receiving unauthorized compensation in their paychecks.

   ○ **Fraud concealment.** The payroll clerk alters the time card to support increased hours, falsely approves a change to the card, or creates a new time card and forges the supervisor's signature.

   ○ **Audit procedure response.** Inspect time cards for signs of alteration and forgeries. Confirm hours paid through interviews of supervisor.

The fraud matrix in Exhibit 4.2 illustrates the fraud penetration analysis focusing on the opportunity to commit the fraud.

Exhibit 4.2   Asset Misappropriation: Fraud Penetration over Time

Company Name
Matrix Fraud Theory and Fraud Audit
Risk Unit: Asset Misappropriation: Fraud Penetration over Time

Fraud: Type/Scheme	Control Opportunity	Occurs/Fraud Scenario	Concealment	Red Flags	Conversion
Embezzlement/ False overtime	Employee	Employee falsely report hours worked. Supervisor unaware of actual hours worked.	Hours worked are falsely recorded. Employee knows no one is watching.	Overtime hours. Consistent pattern of reported hours.	Overstated wages
Embezzlement/ False overtime	Employee and employee	Employees report time for each other. Supervisor unaware of actual hours worked.	Hours worked are falsely recorded. Employees know no one is watching.	Overtime hours. Consistent pattern of reported hours.	Overstated wages
Embezzlement/ False overtime	Employee and supervisor	Supervisor falsely approves hours.	False approval of overtime hours.	Overtime hours. Consistent pattern of reported hours Favoritism.	Employee provides kickback to supervisor
Embezzlement/ False overtime	Employee and payroll	Payroll falsely enters overtime hours into system. Overtime is not evident in department.	Discards actual time card, alters time information or creates a false time card and forges supervisor signature.	Missing time card. Signs of alteration. Differences in handwriting.	Employee provides kickback to supervisor
Embezzlement/ False overtime	Payroll	Payroll falsely enters overtime hours into system. Overtime is not evident in department.	None; employee knows no one is reviewing payroll input.	Overtime hours. Consistent pattern of reported hours. Difference in time card and hours.	Overstated wages

5

Fraud Data Mining

At one time, auditors would examine all the organizational transactions that occurred for the audit period. Today companies process billions of transactions each year. The thought of examining all transactions is mind-boggling. As a result, auditors moved to sampling transactions as a means to test controls and identify fraud. Today, auditors can have the best of both worlds by using fraud data mining to examine the entire population of transactions and to select a sample to test controls and identify fraud.

In the traditional sense, data mining is the use of data extraction software to examine data. However, data mining can also occur through a properly structured interview or the use of judgmental review of accounting journals. Without question, computers are faster at the actual examination of a database. Still, the computer is no replacement for the auditor's skills and professional experience.

Fraud data mining is the process of obtaining and analyzing transactional data to identify anomalies or patterns indicative of a specific fraud scheme. The technique is both analytical and intuitive. It is analytical because it allows for the auditor to link available data to the specific fraud scheme. Intuitively, the auditor interprets the transactions for patterns associated with the fraud scheme.

By analyzing the data in a logical step-by-step manner, a specific fraud scheme inherent to a business system can be recognized. To reach this objective, the first step begins with the application of fraud theory to the data mining plan, this step is followed by: mapping the database to the fraud data profile; use of exclusion and inclusion theory to refine the data; sampling design considerations; and the development of search routines. Consider internet surfing. You start at a Web site, and then link to another Web site, and, then more, until some time later, you have no idea where you are, where you started, and what you found. To use data mining without a logical progression in analyzing the data is a lot like Internet surfing.

In addition, intuition plays a role in data mining because auditors need to use professional judgment in reviewing the data for anomalies and patterns. All the analysis in the world can result in an incomplete data picture without the application of such professional judgment. A common mistake among auditors is to think they can produce one report that will list all the fraudulent transactions. In reality, the process is an ongoing circular process that requires auditors to continually review the data and perform subsequent analyses on it if, in their judgment, such additional review is necessary.

APPLYING FRAUD THEORY

If executed properly, fraud data mining identifies transactions that have a higher propensity of fraud than other transactions. To do so, data mining focuses on both excluding transactions and including transactions. The objective is to find a discrete number of transactions that can be examined using fraud audit procedures. Remember, the goal of fraud auditing is to identify one fraudulent transaction. If one fraudulent transaction is found within this discrete number of transactions, the audit plan will dictate that the sample be expanded.

As explained in Chapter 2, data mining is a part of a fraud audit. The fraud audit is defined as the application of audit procedures to a population of business transactions to facilitate the likelihood of identifying fraud. The first step in the fraud audit is the implementation of the fraud risk assessment to identify the fundamental fraud scheme, also referred to as the inherent fraud risk. Once the inherent fraud scheme or schemes are identified, a fraud data profile for each variation of fraud scheme is developed. In essence, the auditor is drawing a picture of the fraud scenario with data.

The sampling technique used on a population of business transactions to isolate the scheme is called data mining. Therefore, data mining is essentially a way to search for transactions that are consistent with a specific fraud scheme, and the resulting transactions isolated correlate to a data profile of a specific variation of the fraud scheme. The resultant data provide the basis for identifying the fraud scheme variations, concealment strategies and associated red flags, and the fraud opportunity. While the objective of the risk assessment is the development of a fraud scenario, this goal can not be reached without the fraud scheme–specific data being obtained and analyzed.

The recognition that one size does not fit all is an important one to remember in developing the fraud data profile to search for fraudulent transactions. Each fraud scheme variation requires different data. Without properly associating the data to the fraud scheme variation, the data mining falsely excludes transactions.

The eight steps in developing a fraud data mining plan are:

1. Understanding the databases

2. Mapping the database elements to the fraud data profile

3. Applying the exclusion and inclusion theory to the database elements associated with the fraud data profile

4. Performing a data integrity analysis on the database elements associated with the fraud data profile

5. Identifying the opportunities for false positives with the data selected

6. Developing a sampling plan

7. Developing search routines, including:

   ◦ Understanding the common mistakes in developing a data analysis

   ◦ Using business applications for data mining

Understanding the Databases

Databases are collections of organized information. They are comprised of a series of tables that store information in columns and rows. The row of information is a record within the table, and the columns are the fields of information. Since the complete picture is stored in a variety of tables, a critical step for auditors is to understand the relationships between the tables. To do so, auditors must:

- Identify the tables that comprise the database. Meet with the database administrator and learn how the tables are structured. Obtain a copy of the data dictionary describing the table structures and fields in the table.

- Understand the relationships among the tables. Identify the fields that link the tables. These fields are referred to as the primary key and foreign keys.

- Identify the information that comprises the record within each table and the eventual database.

- Identify the information contained in each data column.

- Understand the purpose of each column and the information contained in each column. Keep in mind that the field name was not necessarily created by an accountant. Although the name may sound like the field needed in the fraud audit sense, the information may actually have served a different purpose for the organization.

- Understand how the information is stored in the column. For example, a database has no consistency in which column the street address was recorded. In addition, the zip code was included in the same column as the city and state. Such issues need to be understood in the context of how the data is used by the organization before it can be addressed in the data mining.

- Understand the usefulness of the data. In terms of usefulness in data mining, auditors can perform data integrity analyses, as explained later in the chapter. If the data integrity analyses present limitations inherent to the data recording, the auditors will need to develop strategies to address them.

Mapping the Fraud Data Profile

The mapping process is designed to link data to a fraud scheme variation. The data dictionary, which is a description of the data tables, data fields, and information contained in the fields of the database, is needed before the process can begin. After obtaining the data dictionary, the first step is to categorize the data fields in the following ways:

- **Informational fields (e.g., name and address).** These fields are used in matching analysis and controlling visibility analysis.

- **Transaction control numbers (e.g., purchase order, invoice, or check number).** These fields are used in duplicate analysis, sequential analysis, missing or gaps in transactional numbers, and logic analysis.

- **Dollar amounts.** These fields provide statistical information, analysis at control levels, duplicate amounts, and anomalies in the amounts.

- **Accounting codes (e.g., the account structure for the general ledger focusing on companies, responsibility centers, and specific accounts).** These fields are useful in developing the stratified data models, change analysis, favoritism, and circumvention analysis.

- **Transaction codes.** These fields and the codes contained in them are critical in creating homogenous populations of data, referred to as the stratified data models. The codes identify transaction types, decision-making, categories of data, etc. For example, the code types in the payment field are: Currency; check, wire transfer, or procurement card. The objective is to segregate each payment code into a separate database which is then analyzed for fraud.

Once the fraud profile is mapped to the appropriate data, a search routine can be developed using specific red flags associated with the concealment strategies inherent to the fraud scheme variations recognized in the profile. A connection can be made between the condition of a data field and either the red flags associated with the concealment strategy or the fraud scheme variation itself. The following conditions are examples involving addresses of this connection between the data field and associated fraud potential:

- **No physical address.** Concealing the physical location of the entity through a PO Box or companies that provide postal addresses

- **Missing address.** Indicates control of contact and distribution of checks

- **Duplicate address.** Indicates conflict of interest or false companies

- **Matching address.** Indicates vendor has the same address as employee

Exclusion and Inclusion Theory

Exclusion and inclusion theory is applied in order to create a homogeneous population of transactions for fraud data mining. Exclusion theory is implemented to filter out those transactions not consistent with the fraud scheme. In this way, auditors shrink the population from an unmanageable number to a manageable one. However, to just exclude transactions would leave an incomplete picture of the data. Therefore, inclusion theory is implemented to focus on those transactions, which should be examined from a fraud audit perspective.

Implementing the exclusion principles would eliminate transactions based on the filtering criteria or the fraud theory criteria. Examples using the two criteria for the exclusion of data follows:

- **Filtering criteria.** Understanding the databases and mapping the fraud data profile results in the fraud focus to be on expenditures in service categories. Therefore, all expenditures in non-service general ledger accounts would be excluded from the analysis of data pertaining to the fraud variation. The transactions are not excluded forever, just for the subsequent analysis of service expenditures.

- **Fraud theory criteria.** An expenditure transaction triggered no red flags as defined in the fraud theory. Therefore, the expenditure transaction is excluded from the subsequent analysis of service expenditures.

- **Auditor Judgment.** The auditor has firsthand knowledge of the vendor and on this basis believes the data to be valid. Therefore, the transaction is excluded from analysis.

The inclusion theory would include transactions that are consistent with the red flags defined in the fraud theory. The difficulty in including these transactions is deciding on which red flags to use, and how many red flags are indicative of the fraud scheme. No algebraic formula gives auditors the exact answer. The decision could be based on an arbitrary number of red flags or on the auditor's judgment.

In addition, a transaction could be excluded in one analysis, but included in a different one. The intent is to normalize the data file, so, that a data anomaly becomes more apparent. Discriminating between different analyses provides a logical means for selecting the transactions.

Data Integrity Analysis

Data integrity analysis is important to determine the availability and reliability of information in the database for fraud analysis. The step is intended to determine what and how data is entered. The step also explains how transactions are processed and how controls are applied within the business process. The following examples show the importance of performing the analysis:

- The telephone number was missing from over 50 percent of the vendors in the vendor master file. Since all inquiries with vendors were coordinated through the field project managers, and not with the person responsible for the accounts payable, the phone number field in the database was not deemed important. Therefore, to perform an integrity test on the accounts payable data looking for duplicate telephone numbers or matches to employee numbers would provide limited benefit.

- Vendor invoice numbers were entered inconsistently regarding leading zeros, special symbols, and letters. The lack of consistency in entering the vendor invoice numbers made sorting or analyzing vendor invoice number ranges difficult. Addresses were entered in four different fields with no apparent consistency. Therefore, matching the vendor address to employee address was problematical.

False Positives

Fraud data mining could identify transactions that appear to match the fraud risk, but in fact are not fraudulent. These false positives should be viewed by auditors as a reality of data mining. Two most common false positive occurrences are associated with data integrity issues and true data anomalies. Auditors may experience these types of false positives:

- Two different vendors have the same address. Further review determines that both companies have space in the same office building. This illustrates a true data anomaly.

- The same bank account number is used for two employees with different first and last names. Further review determines the two employees are married, but chose not to change their names. This indicates a true data anomaly.

- One vendor had three different vendor numbers. Further review determines that the addresses were entered as a physical address, a P.O. Box number, and an address from an old location. This situation is indicative of a data integrity issue.

Sampling Design Considerations

Fraud data mining is all about searching for a specific error. The approach to sampling is focused, nonrandom, and biased toward the specific fraud scheme. Therefore, the intent is not to offer an opinion on the effectiveness of the internal controls, but to search for fraudulent transactions. The error searches can be categorized as:

- **Total database searches:** searching the entire database for a specific fraud error. The search for duplicate telephone records for different vendors would be an example of the total database search.

- **Stratified database searches:** normalize or filter the database to those records with a higher propensity to be associated with a specific fraud scheme. A key point is to break the database into the smallest logical units in order to be able to see anomalies within the data. Searching for a front company versus an overbilling scheme would be an example.

- **Fraud routine searches:** design of a search routine focused on a type of error associated with a specific fraud scheme. The key is to understand not only what the search routine will detect, but also the fraud scheme variations that could be missed. Such a search must consider the sophistication of the fraud concealment strategy as described in Chapter 4.

Common Mistakes in Data Analysis

A common mistake in fraud data mining occurs when the auditor thinks of the search routine before defining the fraud scheme. To illustrate the mistake, let's look at matching of the vendor database to the employee database. The objective is to identify fictitious vendors by matching the name, address, telephone number, government identification number, or bank account number to the same information of an employee. Such a matching fails at identifying fraudulent vendors, when the perpetrator has established a unique company or stolen the identity of a real vendor. The reason for the failure is that the sophistication factor of the fraud concealment strategy is ignored.

The data mining plan must consider the dollar magnitude of the fraud scheme. Frauds can be a $1 million transaction or a million $1 transactions. In addition, control systems are often built around dollar levels that equate to a person's responsibility. Individuals usually processed fraudulent transactions below their control threshold. By focusing only on high-dollar transactions, auditors will miss all the smaller-dollar frauds.

The Health South case illustrates the importance of considering dollar magnitude. Specifically, journal entries below a certain dollar level were recorded, thereby, creating a massive overstatement of the financial statements. Therefore, management took advantage of the auditor's materiality levels to misrepresent the financial well being of the company.

Data Mining Using Business Applications

Business applications often have search routines that provide transaction history by vendor, employee, or customer. Therefore, for auditors, business applications can be useful tools to obtain a history of activity or a profile of a vendor, customer, or employee.

For example, overtime fraud is a common scheme within the payroll system. In one fraud audit, a summary of overtime history revealed employees with repeated overtime had overtime pay that exceeded 50 percent of their base salary. By using a business application, in this case, the payroll system, the auditors were able to obtain the weekly history of the noted employees within minutes. Although the same report could have been produced using data extraction software, why re-create the wheel?

THE FRAUD DATA ANALYSIS PLAN

Auditors need a plan to analyze the fraud data. They first must understand the population of transactions using sort and summarize tools. Then they need to search for data patterns consistent with the fraud scheme variation. Developing a plan in this manner avoids haphazard analyses and consequently, unsatisfactory results.

The objective of the analysis is to assist auditors in filtering an audit population of a million transactions down to a smaller group of homogeneous transactions. The analyses work as search engines designed to identify information. The sole function of each one is to identify data patterns, and, then the auditors need to interpret the results. Incorporating the fraud penetration risk assessment in the data analysis plan, as a final step, will result in the flagging of transactions that require scrutiny of the underlying documentation.

The three steps in developing a fraud data analysis plan are:

1. Create homogeneous groups of data.

2. Use analyses to search for fraudulent transactions.

3. Incorporate the fraud penetration risk assessment.

Homogenous Groups of Data

As previously discussed, the first step in the fraud data analysis plan is to understand the data using sort and summarize tools. These tools are defined as follows:

- **Summarize, count, stratify, or classify:** These actions provide statistics concerning the population. The statistics are necessary for the auditors to establish the norms and the extremes. The statistics also provide auditors with the number of accounts or transactions.

- **Sorting:** This tool arranges the data in an ascending or descending order to facilitate the data review, and can be numeric or text-based.

The summary and sort tools enable auditors to understand the audit population and to create smaller homogeneous groups of data. For example, vendor expenditures could be summarized and/or sorted as:

- Cost of sales versus administrative expenditures
- Service expenditures versus tangible goods
- Inventory purchases versus supply purchases
- Expenditures above and below a control threshold

Data Analysis Routines

Data analysis routines are designed to search for data patterns consistent with the identified fraud schemes. Such patterns may include:

- **Missing or gaps:** The search focuses on data fields that have no information or missing transactions due to a missing sequential number. Remember, an overall fraud concealment strategy is to control access or decrease visibility.

- **Duplicate:** This routine is performed to identify entities or transactions containing the same information.

- **Logic tests:** These routines search for transactions that do not fit the norm for the traditional transaction.

- **Circumvention analysis:** This routine searches for transactions below the control threshold and ones that bypass control functions.

- **Matching or compare:** This routine consists of matching the database under audit to other databases not under the control of the perpetrator.

- **Change analysis:** The word "change" is very often associated with fraudulent transactions. The search routine looks for change in identifying information, account activity, and volume of activity.

Fraud Penetration Risk Assessment

The final step in developing the fraud data analysis plan is to incorporate the fraud penetration risk assessment. The fraud penetration risk assessment, as discussed in Chapter 4, uses analysis of the fraud sophistication, the fraud magnitude, and key transactions. Therefore, in terms of the fraud analysis plan, the fraud penetration risk assessment focuses on the following considerations:

- What are the different transaction types?

- What are the scheme variations as to entity and transaction?

- How do the transactions flow through the general ledger accounts?

- Fraud is committed by people. The control opportunity considerations relate to an individual's ability to initiate, process, record, and authorize a transaction.

- The perpetrator's fraud sophistication will have a direct impact in your ability to detect the fraudulent transactions.

- Internal control inhibitors weaken the effectiveness of the internal controls without presenting the appearance of doing so. Auditors will need to use intuitive skills to acknowledge the existence of inhibitors into the data mining plan by developing specific data analysis.

Data Mining Example

Data mining is used in the search for a fraud scheme where a front company is billing for services not provided. Given the specific fraud scheme, the data mining will not target the detection of overbilling, disguised purchases, and conflict-of-interest. Instead, the data mining plan is designed to use analyses associated with a front company scheme.

Employ Sort and Summarize Tools　Start with developing a report that summarizes total vendor dollars and total vendor invoices. The summary would show the amounts sorted high to low, and it includes the calculation of an average invoice amount. The report would provide statistical information regarding dollar volume and transactional volume. Also, the report would list those vendors falling below key control levels.

A second sort is performed where the data is sorted by general ledger account or by vendor with amounts from highest to lowest. The resulting data can then be reviewed to search for vendors used by one manager.

A summary is then prepared for purchase orders by vendor and invoice by vendor. The summary is needed to identify vendors that bypass the purchase order review or vendors having multiple invoices applied to a purchase order.

Apply Exclusion and Inclusion Theory   Using the results from the sort and summarize step, eliminate those vendors that do not appear to be fictitious companies billing for false services. This elimination can start with vendors that auditors know have real companies. If the vendor is a real vendor and is submitting fictitious invoices, other analyses apply pertaining to an overbilling fraud scheme and not the front company scheme being addressed here. After applying the sort and summarize tools and the exclusion and inclusion theory the following conclusions are reached:

- Vendors that are known to the auditor (i.e., vendors that provide attest services to the organization)

- Vendors with a transaction or dollar volume above or below a threshold (i.e., a vendor with one invoice for $934)

Additionally, at this point, an intuitive review would be performed to eliminate those vendors:

- With a high number of invoices: High being relative to the norm for the company and the expense. For example, a cleaning service that bills weekly, results in 52 invoices per year if services are provided each week. If not, then 52 invoices are irrelevant.

- Where the total dollar or total number of invoices is above a threshold: The sole reason to eliminate this data is when the internal controls require two levels of approval.

The intuitive review would include vendors with non-descript names, vendors unknown to the auditor, and vendor invoice patterns that are consistent with the data profile.

Performing Data Analysis Routines   The next step would be to search for patterns consistent with the identified fraud scheme.

Missing Information
- Identify those vendors on the list that have missing identifying information, such as a physical address, telephone number, bank account information, contact person, or government identification number.
- Identify invoices with no purchase order or purchase orders with more than one invoice applied to them.

Duplicate Information
- Identify vendors with duplicate identifying vendor information, such as address, telephone number, bank account information, government identification number, and vendor contact person.
- Identify duplicate invoice numbers or duplicate invoice amounts.

Matching Information
- Identify vendors with matching information to employee or customer database, such as address, telephone number, bank account information, contact person, or government identification number.

Logic Tests
- Identify invoices with sequential invoice numbers or invoice number ranges that appear to be illogical for the vendor.
- Identify invoice amounts that repeat, even-number amounts or odd-number amounts, when even numbers are normal.
- Identify purchase order numbers that either are below or exceed the purchase order range for the audit period.
- Identify invoices where the purchase order date equals or exceeds the vendor invoice date. This would indicate where management is procuring and purchasing is simply creating a purchase order.

Reality of Data Mining   Auditors will need to analyze the information to identify patterns that are indicative of a front company false billing scheme. The eventual goal is a subjective, focused, and bias sample designed to highlight the specific fraud scheme.

Data Mining via the Structured Interview

It could be said that interviewing is the poor man's data mining. However, nothing is further from the truth. Experience has shown that asking the right question in the right way of the right person is a highly effective way to locate fraud.

Interview questions should be structured around the specific fraud scheme identified in the fraud risk assessment. The questions should be directed both at the individuals responsible for the control and others in the organization who maybe able to shed light on the fraud risk.

Example of Data Mining via an Interview   The fraud scheme in this example is known as favored vendors. Inquiries will be made of the purchasing manager; however, regular users of the purchasing function should also be interviewed. These types of questions should be asked of the purchasing manager:

- What is your process for reviewing requisitioned specifications?

- Have you had a disagreement with the requisitioner as to the necessity of the specifications?

- Do you have a problem with a department head specifying brands/vendors for a specific product?

- Is there a review by the legal advisor/officer before the contract is finalized?

- Is there a standard/template contract? If there are deviations from the standards/template, is there provision for review/authorization?

- How are vendors involved in establishing specifications?

- Has senior management interfered, directly or indirectly, in the procurement process? If so, how?

- Has senior management been involved in specification setting or evaluation criteria?

  These are the types of questions to ask of operating management:

- Do you have a problem with a procurement officer trying to lead you to favor one vendor?

- Are there requisitions where you require technical expertise to formulate the specifications?

- Did you get what you asked for, in terms of specifications?

- Has senior management interfered, directly or indirectly, in the procurement process? If so, how?

- Has senior management been involved in specification setting or evaluation criteria?

  The intent of the example above is to illustrate how questions can reveal leads to fraudulent transactions. Some of the most vital fraud findings are found by asking the right question, in the right way, and of the right person.

6

Fraud in Expenditure

Willie Sutton, the famous bank robber, was asked why he robbed banks. He replied: because that is where the money is. In reality, the same answer applies to fraud in the expenditure cycle. Many large-asset misappropriation fraud schemes occur in the expenditure cycle, particularly concerning cash disbursements.

A logical starting point for the search of fraud is in the cash disbursement system. Due to the nature of the cash disbursement schemes, auditors find it easier to identify fraudulent transactions. The reason is that most of the records are accessible to the auditor, unlike, revenue skimming schemes.

When addressing expenditure fraud, the fraud risk assessment clearly starts with the inherent cash disbursement fraud schemes. However, before looking at these schemes more closely, an explanation of front companies is needed given how often their presence is found in schemes involving the expenditure cycle.

FORMATION OF FRONT COMPANIES

A front company, often referred to as a shell company, is a company that has no active business purpose. Therefore, the front company is typically created for the sole purpose of an illegal activity. It exists on paper and, so, characteristically has no physical address, no employees, and does not produce goods or provide services. However, in order to execute fraudulent activity, a front company is legally incorporated, files tax returns, and complies with the required statutory filings within the state of incorporation. Consequently, these companies frequently are used to shield identities and/ or to hide money.

Front companies are used in many of the fraud schemes concerning expenditure fraud, such as false billing and pass-through company schemes. In addition, they facilitate such schemes as those involving a conflict-of-interest, bribery, money laundering, and fraudulent conveyances. Of those schemes just listed, bribery, money laundering, and fraudulent conveyances will be discussed in later chapters, since they typically are not categorized under expenditure fraud. Therefore, before the other schemes can be discussed as categories of expenditure fraud, an understanding of front companies and their use in such schemes is necessary.

Forming a shell entity is a simple process, especially given the number of ways a company can be created. For example, the principal owner of the business, an attorney or individual acting on behalf of the business, or a third-party agent may submit the filings and necessary paperwork to a State for company formation. They can submit by mail, in person, by fax, or online via e-mail. States typically require the following information:

- Company name
- Name and address of agent for service of process
- Number or type of shares (if corporation)
- Names, addresses, or signatures of incorporators or organizers
- Filing fees

Usually a division of the secretary of state's office or another related state agency handles the paperwork. Staff members of the governing agency check for the availability of the desired company name, make sure all required information is listed and completed in the application, and subsequently process the payment. Staff members do not verify information collected from applicants. After the paperwork is complete, the state makes a decision to accept, suspend, or reject the formation.

For a fee, company formation agents will assist individuals with forming a company by filing required documents on their behalf. They can also serve as the agent for service of process, file any periodic reports for the company, and assist in setting up business bank accounts. States that do require a name and address for company formation agents seldom verify their identities. A few states, such as Wyoming, require that formation agents who represent five corporations or more annually register with the appropriate state agency. Agents are subject to the laws of the jurisdictions in which they operate. Formation agents generally do not need any ownership information from their clients, since most states do not require it.

A Criminal's Perspective

Criminals might follow these steps in forming a shell entity for illegal purposes:

1. Search online for a company formation agent. e.g., Agents for Delaware Corporations: http://www.agentsfordelaware.com/FormingACorporation .html.

2. Go to the location of the business and request services in assisting formation of a corporation.

   a. For anonymity, these agents file all necessary paperwork with the state and use one of their executive's names as the incorporator of the corporation.

   b. Agent's fees are paid with cash, money order, or a prepaid credit card in order to guarantee that there is no link to the individual creating the corporation.

   c. Obtain a P.O. Box with post office to establish a company address.

3. Open a bank account at a local bank in the business name with the state-filed documents. Use false documents for identification purposes.

4. Obtain a prepaid cell phone to use as business phone. Such cell phone carriers do not check background information or verify names for prepaid purchases and services.

5. Have some inexpensive business cards printed to imply that the business is legitimate by using only the name of the business, a P.O. Box, and a phone number, and no contact name, no logo, and no e-mail address.

6. Submit invoices to corporate accounts payable function for professional services in accordance with company authorization policies and procedures.

7. Receive payments for professional services invoices and deposit the funds into a business bank account. Preferably, have the payment wired to the bank account.

8. After the checks clear or based on some external event, close the business bank account, discontinue the prepaid cell phone number from service, and close the P.O. Box that you had originally set up for mailing purposes, or let all services expire.

9. Destroy any and all paperwork associated with the professional services company.

10. Move.

Variations of Fictitious Companies

The front company is the starting point for committing the fraud scheme. Several variations of front companies exist.

- **The company does not exist.** The perpetrator knows that no independent verification of the new vendor occurs.

- **The company was created legally but does not function like a true company.** The perpetrator creates the legal shell, obtains a government identification number, sets up a bank account in the name of the corporation, and obtains a telephone number. In a more sophisticated scheme, the perpetrator rents an office and has an employee answering the telephone.

- **The company is real, but a false address or bank information is provided.** The real company is not conducting business with your company. The perpetrator steals the identity of the real company, establishes a bank account in the real company's name, and negotiates the checks or accepts wire transfers.

- **The company is real, but it is dormant as to doing business with your company.** At one time the vendor did business with your company. Since the vendor is on the master file, the perpetrator changes the address or bank account number of the dormant vendor.

- **Look-alike, similar name, multi-account vendor.** Due to the similar name, the vendor appears to be a real company.

- **Temporary vendors/limited use.** It is not uncommon to have no vendor verification procedures for vendors that will receive only one payment. The perpetrator submits for payment one invoice per temporary vendor.

The fraud matrix in Exhibit 6.1 illustrates the application of fraud theory to a false billing scheme using front company variations.

Data Mining for Front Companies

The key attributes are the name, address, telephone number, government identification number, contact person, and bank account number. The search on the vendor identity would focus on matching to employee databases or missing key attributes as a way to maintain control over contacting the vendor.

The name of the company is usually a common or nondescript one. The objective is to ensure that the name of the front company does not arouse curiosity. The address is a nonphysical address, such as a post office box. The telephone number could be a cell phone number or a number answered by an answering service. Unsophisticated perpetrators may use their own home address and home telephone number. Auditors should never assume that perpetrators use a high degree of sophistication to conceal the fraud scheme.

The search for fictitious vendor invoices focuses on the invoice amount, invoice dates, frequency of invoices, and the sequencing of invoice numbers.

Exhibit 6.1   False Billing Scheme Using a Front Company

Company Name
Matrix of Fraud Theory and Fraud Audit
Risk Unit: Fraud Penetration Front Company and False Billing

Scheme Variation/ Control Opportunity	Control Opportunity	Occurs/Fraud Scenario	Concealment	Red Flags	Conversion
Company is not legally created	Operating management	Remote likelihood of occurring due to new vendor controls; Temporary vendor scenario	None; No one is looking; Volume of activity; Temporary vendor status	New company; Company not recognized by managers; See document red flags matrix.	Negotiate payment in front company bank account.
Company is legally created but does not function as true company	Operating management	Properly approved invoice for new vendor; Company passes vendor registration; Invoice does not require receiving report;	Front company; False invoices; False approval; Nonperformance of control procedure; No invoice supporting charge	New company; Address or bank account match to employee; See document red flags matrix.	Negotiate payment in front company bank account.
	Accounts payable	Expenditure recorded in responsibility center that does not have a detailed review of charges to center			

Exhibit 6.1 False Billing Scheme using a Front Company (*continued*)

Company Name
Matrix of Fraud Theory and Fraud Audit
Risk Unit: Fraud Penetration Front Company and False Billing

Scheme Variation/ Control Opportunity	Control Opportunity	Occurs/Fraud Scenario	Concealment	Red Flags	Conversion
Dormant vendor; Change address or bank account	Accounts payable; Operating management	False request submitted for change; Forged approvals; Invoice does not require receiving report.	False invoices; False approval; False address change or bank account	Change from dormant to active; Change of bank account or address; See document red flag matrix.	Negotiate payment in front company bank account
Real company's identity used	Operating management; Accounts payable	Same as legally created fictitious company; Failure to validate physical address	False invoices; False approval; False address change or bank account	Same company name with different addresses; See document red flag matrix.	Negotiate payment in front company bank account
Look-alike company/ Multi-account vendor	Operating management; Accounts payable	Same as legally created fictitious company; Failure to validate physical address	False invoices; False approval; False address change or bank account	New vendor; Local address or bank account; See document red flag matrix.	Negotiate payment in front company bank account
Temporary vendor	Operating management; Accounts payable	No vendor validation due to one-time payment control; Relies on manager approval of invoice	False invoices; False approval; False address change or bank account	Same address or bank account information as other temporary vendors; See document red flag matrix.	Negotiate payment in front company bank account

General Ledger Considerations	Transaction Considerations	Fraud Magnitude Considerations	Internal Control Inhibitors Considerations	Fraud Audit Methodology	Fraud Audit Awareness
1. Service expenditure categories	1. No purchase order or open purchase order	1. Tends not to exceed 52 transactions a week	1. Management override	1. Focus on front company indicators	1. See document red flag matrix
2. Department-specific supplies	2. Expenditures with no independent receiving	2. Exception is cost of goods, if no inventory control	2. Logical collusion	2. Focus on patterns in invoice numbers, dates and amounts	2. Vendors used by one manager
3. Cost of sales if no independent receiving report	3. Sequential or illogical vendor invoice number	3. Expenditure by vendor less than $1,000	3. Failure to independently verify representation of vendor information	3. Data mining focus on each vendor variation	3. Commonality of invoice amounts
			4. Overreliance on manager approval	4. Data mining focus on change and match to address and bank account	4. Vendor variations

A review of invoice sequencing centers on sequential numbering, any range of numbers that are illogical for the vendor, or a common set of integers in the number. An analysis of invoice amounts entails looking at even invoice amounts, amounts below but near control thresholds, and duplicate amounts. In addition, the overall invoice search would correlate purchase orders to vendor invoices. Looking a purchase orders, the specific data to focus on would be a purchase order number, amount, and date. Auditors should pay particular attention to invoices without a purchase order or invoices applied to an open purchase order. The lack of purchase order matching invoices decreases the visibility of the invoice within the accounts payable control function. A purchase order date that is the same or later than invoice date would identify managers circumventing the purchasing control process.

Additional searches would target payment information, specifically, payment amount, payment date, and check number. This data can reveal preferential payment schemes. For example, if the payment date is the same as the invoice date, an override situation might exist. To test for such a situation, auditors need to focus on invoices that are paid more quickly than the normal payment terms. If invoices are paid in 30 days, why is the ABC Company consistently paid in 10 days? One possible explanation is that the ABC Company is owned by a company employee.

Audit Steps for Front Companies

Fraud auditing procedures require the auditor to obtain evidence not under the control of the perpetrator. The idea is to obtain evidence from independent sources to confirm or refute the auditor's suspicions. These nine audit steps are designed to support or refute these suspicions.

1. Contact the vendor via telephone. A pattern of telephone calls being answered by an answering service or answering machine increases the likelihood of a front company.

2. Visit the vendor's Web site. The lack of a Web site is uncommon for real companies.

3. Determine that the front company is legally incorporated.

4. Compare the first payment date to the front company with the front company's incorporation date. If the incorporation date is within 90 days of the payment date, consider the front company to be suspicious.

5. Determine if the front company is recognized by competitors or other subsidiaries.

6. Determine if the front company is recognized by other members of management.

7. Determine if the front company has membership in any legitimate business associations.

8. Determine if the front company has secured debt recorded at a government office.

9. Perform a site visit of the front company.

SYNOPSIS OF FRAUD SCHEMES

Given the extent of expenditures for a given business, it is not surprising that many fraud schemes would arise with regard to them. The following section provides in-depth discussion of several categories of the most prominent of these schemes.

False Billing Schemes

In false billing schemes, people pay for goods or services that are not delivered, and the company is a fictitious one. The scheme is concealed through a false invoice, false approvals by the manager, and variations of front companies. The conversion occurs by payments to bank accounts in the name of the front company that is controlled by the perpetrator of the scheme. False billing schemes can also be committed by a real company in collusion with a company employee. In the scheme, an employee would receive a kickback from the real company. False billing schemes have been used to pay the bribe tax as described in Chapter 8.

Red Flags of False Billing Schemes   In the test of controls and the examination of documents, auditors need to be alert to observable events that would cause them to suspect fraud. While no one red flag may cause auditors to launch an investigation, a combination of events should cause an increased awareness. It is recommended that auditors develop the red flag matrix as shown in Chapter 2. A list of common red flags of suspicious vendor transactions follows.

Document Condition
- Lack of fold marks or fold marks that should not exist
- Data mailer invoices that have no carbon spots
- Document condition appears new
- Documents torn or missing parts
- Documents missing key information
- Copies or drafts of documents
- Only photocopies of documents exist
- Signs of alteration, overwriting, or counterfeiting

- Handwritten information
- Signs of cutting and pasting
- Missing documents
- Illogical paper type
- Paper stock or printing not consistent with that used in a company of similar size
- Type font not consistent with that found in a company of similar size

Vendor Invoices
- Missing logical information for the goods and services, e.g., purchase order number, delivery locations
- Missing logical additional charges: sales tax, value added tax (VAT), or shipping and handling
- Produced from low-cost business software
- Produced from word processing software
- A copy or a fax copy
- Information is incorrect, e.g., arithmetic accuracy, purchase order number not in logical range or duplicate number
- Electronic invoices with user ID information matching company ID information

Transaction Control Data
- Invoice numbers are sequential over a period of time
- Invoice number range is not consistent with perceived company size
- No purchase order number is associated with payment
- One purchase order is associated with many payments

Missing Information
- No telephone number
- No physical address
- No contact person
- No government identification number
- No company Web site
- No company tagline or logo

- Missing industry standard information
- No membership in like business or trade groups

Illogical Changes or Occurrences
- Vendor used only by one manager or subsidiary
- Geographic distance between the operating location and the vendor
- First payment date is in close proximity to incorporation date of the front company
- Changes to vendor address or bank account information
- Dormant vendors that become active

Overbilling on Invoices

Overbilling schemes differ from false billing schemes in that the vendor is a real vendor and actual goods or services are provided. The real vendor typically commits the scheme in collusion with a company employee. The real vendor over charges the company and an accounts payable manager approves the vendor invoice for payment. The vendor can commit the scheme without internal collusion by taking advantage of known internal control weaknesses. Overbilling on a vendor invoice occurs in these ways:

- Fictitious charges on fictitious invoices
- Overcharging on price
- Charging for a higher quantity than delivered
- Charging for a higher quality than delivered (product substitution)
- Charging for goods/services that are not needed by the company
- Including false or inflated charges on real invoices

The concealment strategy is employed by the vendor overcharging on the invoice, because of known weaknesses in the company's receiving or approval process or in collusion with a company employee in the receiving or approval process. Tolerances built into accounts payable to pay invoices within a percent of the original purchase order would allow the scheme to occur without internal involvement.

The conversion occurs through kickbacks from the vendor or the vendor retaining the overcharged amount.

Data Mining for Overbilling   Data mining for overbilling varies by the type of the overbilling scheme and the nature of the general ledger accounts.

Overbilling schemes can be difficult to search for electronically due to their nature. For example, a product substitution case would not necessarily be visible when reviewing the electronic file. The level of detail captured in the accounting system usually does not allow for recognition of overbilling. Traditionally, a vendor invoice is entered by total, so, there is no line-by-line description of the invoice. As a result, other data mining techniques should be considered.

Depending on the magnitude and frequency of the scheme, one effective technique is the use of a block sample from a period of time. In addition, interviewing of employees using the goods or services can help auditors identify overbilling schemes.

Audit Procedures for Overbilling   The nature of overbilling requires auditors to conduct a separate fraud audit procedure for each scheme variation. The audit procedure is tailored to the nature of the goods or services. An illustration follows.

Illustration of the Overbilling Audit Program   Assume that your company has a fleet of automobiles that require periodic maintenance and repairs. Your company has outsourced the repair service to the ABC service company. Each time a car enters the repair facility, a pre-numbered multipart service request form is completed. The purpose of the form is to document the nature of the service, provide authorizations, the requisition for parts, and the eventual payment approval of the invoice. The form is also sent to the transportation department which maintains a repair history for each automobile.

The terms of the service agreement state the hourly rate for the mechanic is $90 and the hours billed are according to the standard rate manual.

The invoice approval process starts with a department employee who matches the work order to the vendor invoice. The procedure is evidenced by a checkmark. Then the service manager reviews and approves the vendor invoice. Lastly, the invoice is forwarded to accounts payable for payment. Exhibit 6.2 illustrates the process of applying fraud theory and the development of the fraud audit response concerning an overbilling scheme. The chart shows the process of associating fraud theory principles on a scheme-by-scheme basis to the appropriate audit response.

Conflicts-of-Interest

In a conflict-of-interest scheme, a company's purchasing officer has a hidden direct or indirect ownership in a vendor from which the company purchases goods or services. The conversion occurs through hidden profits obtained via the ownership interest. The scheme does not always result in losses for the company, but it is almost always against company policies.

Exhibit 6.2   Overbilling Fraud Audit Matrix

Company Name
Matrix Fraud Theory and Fraud Audit
Risk Unit: Asset Misappropriation: Overbilling

Fraud: Type/Scheme	Control Opportunity	Occurs/Fraud Scenario	Concealment	Red Flags	Conversion
Vendor invoice contains one or more false charges	Vendor and manager; Vendor and administrator	False work order prepared; Management override	False work order —Counterfeit —Altered or real work order Valid VIN # on work order	Work order appearance Handwriting or ink type	Kickback to manager or administrator
Invoice rate exceeds contract amount	Vendor and manager	False statement on rate —After-hours repair —Weekend repair	False approval of rate	Condition not consistent with contract	Kickback to manager
Invoice standard hours greater than rate book	Vendor and manager	Vendor knows standard hours are not verified	None Hours are not verified	Even hours; Hours appear high	Kickback to manager
Service performed was not required	Vendor and manager	Mechanic representation	Work order indicates repair necessary	History of repairs —By auto —By repair	Kickback to manager
Mechanic provided does not have proper qualifications	Vendor	Vendor misrepresents qualifications	False qualifications on resume	No specific red flag	Vendor retains overcharge
Repair on noncompany vehicle	Manager	Manager allows noncompany vehicle to be repaired	False ID #, plate, and description of vehicle; Information on work order altered.	Part type not consistent with fleet; Repair on vehicle in use	Manager charges nonemployee and retains fee

Exhibit 6.2 Overbilling Fraud Audit Matrix (*continued*)

Company Name
Matrix Test of Fraud Red Flags
Risk Unit: Asset Misappropriation: Overbilling

Fraud Scheme	Sampling Strategy	Data-Mining Strategy	Test of Controls Audit Procedure	Fraud Audit Procedure	Fraud Conclusion
Vendor invoice contains one or more false charges	Data mining	Frequency of repair by: —Vehicle —Type of repair —Mechanic —Vehicle assigned and nonassigned	See Audit Program Step 7	Determine that corresponding part purchased; Determine if vehicle was in use day of service	
Invoice rate exceeds contract amount	Block sample month of September	Database does not capture information	See Audit Program Step 7	Independently verify representation for higher rate	
Invoice standard hours greater than rate book	Block sample month of September	Database does not capture information	See Audit Program Step 7	Compare hours on invoice to hours in rate manual	
Service performed was not required	Data mining	See Data Mining for false charge	See Audit Program Step 7	For assigned vehicles, interview user as to known problems	
Mechanic provided does not have proper qualifications	Complete population of all mechanics	None	See Audit Program Step 7	Interview mechanic as to qualifications; Compare to resume	
Repair on noncompany vehicle	Block sample month of September	See Data Mining for false charge	See Audit Program Step 7	Verify part # consistent with fleet	

The perpetrator has a beneficial rather than a legal ownership interest where they receive a disguised payment for directing the business relationship to the conflict-of-interest company. The payment could be described as a kickback, but the intent of the transaction is different from the traditional kickback scheme.

Data Mining for Conflicts-of-Interest Schemes   Inherently no specific data mining procedures identify conflict-of-interest schemes. Auditors could be guided by past published schemes, such as ownership in real estate schemes. Tips and rumors concerning close relationships or managers insisting on the use of a particular vendor are useful in identifying conflicts of interest. In addition, data mining front companies may reveal conflict of interests.

Audit Procedure for Conflicts-of-Interest Schemes   The audit procedure determines the beneficial owner of the corporation. The beneficial owner may be revealed through examining these records:

- Examine incorporation records at a state's Secretary of State's office.

- If the entity is a limited liability company, request the right to inspect copies of the tax returns.

- If the entity is a corporation, request the right to inspect stock records.

- Request counsel for the questioned entity to provide confirmation of the entity's owners or shareholders.

Pass-Through Company Schemes

Pass-through company schemes use a front company also. The schemes are a combination of false billing, overbilling, and conflict-of-interest schemes. The mechanics of the scheme are:

- A purchasing manager establishes a front company.

- A real company procures goods or services from the pass-through front company.

- The pass-through front company purchases the items from a real vendor in the marketplace.

- The real vendor provides the goods and services to a company and bills the pass-through front company. In a more sophisticated scheme, the goods are delivered to the front company first, and then the front company ships the goods. A freight forwarding company facilitates the scheme.

- The front company submits an invoice to a company at a markup from the real vendor.

The scheme can also occur with services, where the front company subcontracts with a real service provider. The front company submits an invoice, which is typically approved by the operating or purchasing manager. Pass-through vendors may be used to procure a single item or a wide range of unrelated items. In the single-item scheme, the company usually purchases the item in large quantities. An example of a multi-item scheme is a front company procuring different items, such as office supplies, equipment, jet fuel, and food items. Thus, the pass-through company scheme can occur in several different variations.

The conversion cycle in the scheme occurs by the pass-through company marking up the real vendors' costs and skimming the profits.

Data Mining for Pass-Through Companies   The search for a pass-through vendor is a difficult process. One approach is to analyze vendor invoices with a wide range of commodity codes or a wide range of charges to different general ledger accounts. Even more difficult to find is the pass-through company that provides one product or service in a large quantity. Since a pass-through vendor is a front company, the data mining for a front company would apply.

Audit Procedure for Pass-Through Company   The key to developing audit procedures to reveal front companies is to focus on determining the true identity of the vendor providing the actual goods or services. The following procedures are designed to reveal a vendor's identity:

- Perform audit procedures for front companies.

- Examine shipping documents or bills of lading that would indicate the true vendor name or the true shipping location.

- Interview employees performing the service as to the identity of their employer.

Disguised Purchases

In the disguised purchases scheme, the need or use of the item is falsely described. The intent of the expenditure is to enrich the employee's lifestyle. There are three primary variations of the scheme.

1. The company employee purchases goods or services that are personal in nature and provide no useful business purpose. The employee subsequently diverts the item to personally benefit from it.

2. The quantity exceeds the company's needs, and the employee enjoys the use of the excess items.

3. The company employee intentionally procures items in excess of company needs and then diverts the items for eventual resale. The scheme

differs from a theft scheme because the employee intends to divert the item at time of procurement. He or she is also responsible for the usage and budgeting of the items. In a theft scheme, an employee diverts the item due to opportunity created by poor physical security controls. The variances or missing items should be an immediate clue for responsible managers.

In a small company, the concealment strategy may be as simple as the fact that no one is looking. The expenditure often mirrors expenditures typically incurred by the company, e.g., cell phone, utilities, auto expenses, or credit card expenditures. In larger companies, the expenditure is within the manager's authorization level. The items diverted are either embedded within an actual business purchase or a theft of the entire purchased item or service. The audit plan needs to focus on items that would logically have a personal benefit. Company events, promotional meetings, employee awards, customer giveaways, computer supplies, and personal services can all present disguised purchase fraud opportunities.

The conversion cycle in both small and large companies is a variation of disguised compensation. The concealment strategies have included paying bribes to customers, politicians, and other decision makers.

The fraud matrix in Exhibit 6.3 illustrates the development of a fraud audit program for the preceding fraud schemes. Unlike previous matrixes, this one illustrates the audit program, not the fraud theory.

Company Procurement Cards

A procurement card is a credit card. It provides an individual the ability to procure goods and services directly from a vendor. Card companies have built into procurement cards several controls to prevent misuse and monitoring reports to detect fraud. Nevertheless, procurement card fraud occurs often in companies.

The procurement card fraud schemes generally correlate to fraud in an expenditure cycle, e.g., disguised purchases, purchase for personal use, excess purchases for resale, fictitious charges in which the vendor provides a kickback to the employee. Use of procurement cards is a target-rich area for fraud auditors.

The concealment strategies are based on the sheer volume of transactions, the difficulty in reviewing the source documents, the fact that the charge is related to the employee's duties, and vendors participating in the scheme.

Diversion of Payment

Diversion of Payment schemes can take place when an employee is able to obtain a check directly from accounts payable or instruct accounts payable to transfer the payment to a bank account or postal address under the

Exhibit 6.3   Asset Misappropriation Disbursement Fraud Schemes

Company Name
Matrix Fraud Audit Response
Risk Unit: Asset Misappropriation: Disbursement Fraud Schemes

Fraud: Type/Scheme	Control Procedure	Concealment	Red Flags	Test of Controls Audit Procedure	Fraud Audit Procedure
Front companies/False billing	Approval of invoices in accordance with company policy	Front company; False invoices; False approval; Nonperformance of control procedure	New company; Document red flag matrix	Examine invoice for proper approvals; Examine documents for appropriateness	Confirm vendor existence; Obtain independent evidence goods or services provided
Front company/ Pass-through scheme	Approval of invoices in accordance with company policy	Front company; Nondisclosure of real company	Shipping documents indicate real company; Variety of items purchased from one company	Examine invoice for proper approvals; Examine documents for appropriateness	Confirm vendor's existence; Determine source of shipments
Vendor overbilling; Product substitution	Invoice approval; Accounts payable match purchase order and receiving report	False approval; Accounts payable accepts manager's approval	Budget variances; Override field on accounts payable; Notes by accounts payable on inquiry; Difference between invoice, purchase order, and receiving report	Examine invoice for proper approvals; Examine documents for appropriateness	Product substitution; Physical inspection of item

Disguised purchases	Approval of invoices in accordance with company policy	Purchase below control threshold; Requires one approval	Items purchased have personal benefit; Manager defensive concerning purchased items	Examine invoice for proper approvals; Examine documents for appropriateness	Independent confirmation of use of item; Logic test of total use of item; Physical inspection of item
Misuse of asset	Assets under control of manager as course of normal duties	Use of asset not on company premises; False representation as to use; False entry in logbook	Defensiveness by manager; Asset stored off site	Ask manager as to use of assets	Surprise inspection of asset during nonworking hours
Lack of business purpose/ Excessive expenditures	Approval of invoices in accordance with company policy	Expenditure within budget; False representations regarding use and need	Nature of item has no logical connection to department; Potential personal use	Examine invoice for proper approvals; Examine documents for appropriateness	Interview employees as to use of asset; Inspect asset to confirm location; Prepare report of items for board audit committee
Conflict of interest	New vendor validation procedures; Conflict-of-interest policy	Legal ownership not disclosed on public documents	None	Examine invoice for proper approvals; Examine documents for appropriateness	Media search; Request inspection of stock certificate ledger

control of the employee. The conversion occurs through the theft of the check or diversion of the wire transfer. These schemes may occur when:

- A manager requests that a check is returned in order to send additional documentation with it.

- The nature of the check requires that it be sent to the operations manager. The settlement of a claim against the company would fit an established pattern.

- Checks returned because of a faulty address are stolen.

- Stale or old checks that have not cleared the bank are stolen. The perpetrator reissues the checks in their name for the same amount or creates counterfeit checks for the same amount.

- Contracted purchasing rebates are diverted.

Employee Reimbursed or Directed

The employee requests expense reimbursements for expenditures that are fictitious or for personal use items. These frauds are typical in moving expenses, fringe benefit programs, travel & entertainment, and petty cash funds. The concealment strategy is to create or alter documentation. In regard to fringe benefit, often companies allow employees to submit copies of receipts rather than originals. However, in one scheme the employee altered original receipts by scanning the receipt into his computer. The alteration was performed electronically, and a new receipt was printed. The conversion occurs through the employee obtaining improper reimbursement.

Accounts Payable Schemes

In these schemes, the accounts payable employees simply disburse funds to themselves, a fictitious company, or in collusion with a real company. The conversion occurs through directing the payment to a controlled address or bank account or through a kickback by a real vendor. Poor password controls procedures allow this scheme to occur even when segregation of duties is built into the password security system.

Another such scheme occurs when the accounts payable function intentionally pays a valid vendor invoice twice. The employee requests the overpayment from the company and diverts the refund or transfers the payment to a self-controlled account.

The flip-flop scheme occurs when accounts payable changes the address of a real vendor to an address controlled by an accounts payable employee. A payment is directed to the address controlled by the perpetrator. The address is changed back after the false payment in order to conceal the fraud. In another scheme, vendor credits are intentionally misapplied to a vendor that is willing to pay the accounts payable employee a kickback.

Credit balances in accounts receivable can be falsely disbursed. Typically, the scheme is initiated by those employees with access to customer information. In such schemes, internal employees surfing the customer account file identify old, unapplied customer credits or aged credit balances. In the old, unapplied credit scheme, the credit is transferred to a customer account controlled by the perpetrator. Similarly, in the aged credit balance scheme, the perpetrator submits a false letter requesting a change to the dormant customer's address. A second false letter is submitted at a later date requesting a refund of the credit balance.

Company payments to a valid vendor are subsequently transferred to a source controlled by the perpetrator. For example, the controller establishes a personal credit card at the same bank as the company credit card. A payment is first directed to the company credit card account. After this payment is posted, thereby, creating the audit trail on the vendor documentation, the controller directs the vendor to transfer the payment to their personal credit card account.

Check-Tampering Schemes

Internal check-tampering schemes occur when an individual obtains physical access to a check through the preparation process, by intercepting the check, or through theft of the check. Parties external to the organization can also tamper with checks, but that variation is beyond the scope of this text.

Most companies have controls and procedures to prevent internal check tampering, but logical and illogical exceptions provide easy opportunity for internal check tampering. Auditors need to ensure that all bank accounts are identified; all check signers are known, as are all special handling procedures.

Both large and small companies are prone to check-tampering schemes at the check preparation stage. Manual check preparation systems exist in companies of all sizes to allow for immediate payment of expenses, e.g., payroll, freight, and claims adjustment and of functions, such as petty cash. The preparer of the check is often the signer and the person responsible for account coding. In one large investigation firm, for example, a special bank account had been established to pay for covert investigation expenses. The request for replenishment of the fund followed all corporate procedures, but the special bank account was completely controlled by the office manager, by being in charge of writing the checks, depositing funds, and reconciling the bank account. The corporation did not have the special bank account recorded in their corporate general ledger.

How check tampering occurs varies as much as the processes for preparing the check. Remember; where there is a will, there is a way.

Check interception schemes can be as simple as coding the check for special handling, returning it to a department head, or simply picking up the check. These opportunities are not always defined in the procedures because of accommodations or personal requests. In one case, checks for personal injury settlements were given directly to the risk manager, who was creating fictitious claims and falsely endorsing the checks.

Check-tampering schemes occur due to one or a combination of these techniques:

- Alteration at time of preparation

- Altering the check after preparation

- Theft of check

- False endorsements or forged signature on front of check

- Signature through trickery

Check-Tampering Occurring in the Preparation Process
- In a manual system, the scheme may be as simple as writing a correct vendor's name or address in the disbursement journal and listing a different name or address on the check.

- Flip-flopping in check preparation occurs when the accounts payable clerk has access to the vendor master file and the vendor input file. The clerk alters the address or bank account information for a vendor on the master file. The check is prepared and mailed to the false address. Then the system address is changed back to the original address, thereby concealing the fraud scheme.

Check-Tampering after Preparation and Involving Proper Signatures
- One such scheme is altering or adding account number information. The payment is to an authorized vendor. However, the accounts payable clerk has a personal account at the same vendor. The clerk adds the personal account number to the check rather than the company's account number.

- The payee name, as printed on the check, is altered after check preparation and the signature process through the use of bleach or erasable ink.

Theft of Check and False Endorsement   Check theft occurs through the theft of checks and falsely endorsing checks. These situations provide the opportunity:

- Theft of stale checks
- Theft of returned checks due to non-deliverable address
- Theft of refund checks mailed to the company
- Theft of blank checks

Signature through Trickery   The signature on the check is the actual signature of the approver. The fraud perpetrator tricks the approver by providing false documentation or gets the approver to sign a blank check based on a false representation.

Check Tampering Audit Response   Absent examining the front and the back of checks, auditors have no firsthand knowledge of the payee or the endorsing party. Therefore, auditors should request and examine four areas on checks:

1. **Payee line.** Ensure the payee on the check matches name on the supporting documentation and entry in the cash disbursement journal. Also, examine the payee line for evidence of tampering or the addition of information.
2. **Examine the signature line.** Ensure the approver is authorized and the signature appears genuine. Compare the signature on the check to a genuine handwriting sample.
3. **Endorsement.** Ensure that the payee endorsed the check. Doing this may be as simple noting the signature to confirming the payee's bank account information.
4. **Additional information.** Ensure that information was not added to the check after the initial preparation. Differences in type or handwriting would be a red flag.

Small-Business Fraud Schemes

Auditors should be aware that there are fraud schemes involving cash disbursements that are typically associated with small businesses. The four most common small-business fraud schemes are:

1. **Unrecorded disbursement.** The bookkeeper writes a check that is not recorded in the cash disbursement journal. The returned check is destroyed. The totals on the cash disbursement journal are falsely inflated to conceal the unrecorded check.

2. **False entry.** The entry on the cash disbursement journal does not match the name on the check. In a manual system, the fraud occurs by simple process of writing a valid vendor's name in the register. In a small-business system, the vendor's name in the register is changed after the creation of the check.

3. **False endorsement.** Someone endorses the back of a check made payable to a legitimate vendor. The owner receiving the bank statement could minimize these frauds by inspecting canceled checks or the images of canceled checks. The auditor can identify this fraud by examining the canceled checks.

4. **Added Information.** Examine the check for evidence of information after the original preparation of the check.

7

Contract Fraud

The good news is that we have a contract documenting the terms and conditions between two parties. The bad news is that we have a contract documenting its terms and conditions between two parties. A contract between two parties is a common business transaction. The intent of the contract is to clearly convey its terms and conditions. In reality, the wording of the contract is both a blessing and a curse.

The fraud audit process begins with the terms and conditions of the contract. Contract fraud can be established through:

- False representations in the billing documents or the underling documents and records: in essence, an overbilling scheme

- False interpretations of the contract

- Building arguments that show the interpretation of the contract is false or misleading

- Other fraud theories related to contract law

CONTRACT FRAUD AUDIT PLAN STEPS

The audit plan for contract fraud is based on the terms and conditions in the contract. The seven steps to developing the audit plan are:

1. Read the contract and the associated documents, rules, and regulations.

2. Identify the pertinent terms and conditions.

3. Develop a common understanding of the terms and conditions.

4. Understand the terms and conditions unique to the industry.

5. Understand the fraud profit motivation.

6. Ensure the audit team is aware of the fraud schemes by preparing a fraud risk assessment of the relevant inherent fraud scheme.

7. Based on the contract type and fraud profit motivation, develop audit strategies for the fraud schemes.

The first step is simply to read the contract. Auditors must have a thorough understanding of the contract terms and conditions, and the understanding must be consistent with that of the supporting legal team. Unless other fraud, such as fraud in the inducement or promissory fraud, can be established, the audit process begins with the wording of the contract. Auditors should be alert for these contract clauses:

- *"Whereas" clauses* reference documents that are incorporated into the contract by reference.

- *Right to audit clauses* defines what accounting records are available for inspection.

- *Record retention clauses* define what records are retained and the length of time the records are required for retention.

- *Pertinent terms and conditions clauses* are the contract terms and conditions relevant to the administration of the contract. Auditors must be aware of:

    ○ Pertinent terms and conditions associated with the charging of costs

    ○ Pertinent terms and conditions associated with contract deliverables

    ○ Key definitions in the contract associated with terms and conditions and the charging of costs

Understanding the Fraud Profit Motivation

The fraud assessment starts with linking the fraud theory to the nature and type of the contract. Fraud profit motivation can be linked to the contract type in the following ways:

- **Fixed price contract.** Since the cost of the contract is fixed, the only remaining fraud profit opportunity is to provide nonconforming goods or services or defective pricing. The use of change orders or contract extensions is common way to inflate the actual costs of a fixed price contract.

- **Cost contract.** The contractor is providing a tangible product and charging for those costs based on a defined methodology in the contract. The contractor receives a markup, referred to as a management fee or an overhead charge, based on direct costs. The fraud focus is on where the costs are incurred, and how the costs are assigned and ultimately charged to the contract. The overcharging can occur through false charges, inflating actual costs, or an overbilling variation. The dishonest contractor is motivated by increasing direct costs to earn a higher management fee.

- **Royalty contract.** The fraud audit considers the basis for calculating the sales unit, the sales dollars, or recording sales activity in an undisclosed set of books. The fraudulent activity is the underreporting of sales or sales through an undisclosed account.

- **Service contract.** The contractor is providing a service and charging for that service based on a defined methodology in the contract. The fraud audit question is whether the service unit occurred as stated in the contract.

The Intent Factor

Once an overbilling scheme is identified or the red flags of the schemes are noted, the next step of the fraud audit is to determine an intent factor. To establish that the overbilling was fraudulent, auditors must have clear and objective criteria to establish the intent of the overbilling scheme. *Black's Law Dictionary* defines intent as the "state of mind accompanying an act, [especially] a forbidden act. While motive is the inducement to act, intent is the mental resolution or determination to do it. When the intent to do an act that violates the law exists, motive becomes immaterial."

As with any legal premise, there are various forms of intent, such as constructive intent, criminal intent, and implied intent. Auditors need to understand the various types in order to know how to develop their observations. Working closely with legal counsel should assist the auditors in this regard.

Guidance from Legal Sources   The False Claim Act within the federal law provides the following guidance on establishing the intent:

- Actual knowledge of the false information
- Acts in deliberate ignorance of the truth or falsity of the information
- Acts in reckless disregard of the truth or falsity of the information

Auditors should meet and obtain legal counsel in order to establish the intent factor of the fraud scheme.

Building the Intent Argument   Building the intent argument is showing that the parties had knowledge or should have had knowledge that the actions of the contractor were intended to conceal the truth. Auditors should consider these sources:

- **Prior administration of the contracts with the same or similar contract language.** Inconsistent administration without cause can be used to show intent.

- **Benching off industry-related practices.** Auditors compare the administration of the contract to accepted industry practices. For example, in the advertising industry, a standard practice is to obtain tearsheets in support of a media placement in a newspaper or magazine. The lack of maintaining standard industry documentation would illustrate the intent of the party to falsely charge, especially, when the media source provides the document to the contractor.

- **Authorities' sources.** Industry trade associations publish statistics, studies, and other information regarding industry best practices. These sources can be useful.

- **Prior audit results.** Audits place individuals on notice concerning internal controls, documentation concerns, and other adjustments. If the individual has a record of prior problems, auditors reviewing prior audit results may establish a reckless disregard theory.

SYNOPSIS OF CONTRACT FRAUD SCHEMES

Overcharging of contracts occurs through honest errors or through fraud. The difference between overcharging and fraud is the intent to conceal the overcharging of the contract. The inherent schemes provide the overall structure for contract fraud schemes. Within each inherent scheme are several variations, depending on the type and nature of the contract.

- **Defective pricing.** The contractor submits false or inaccurate information regarding costs or prices in reference to the performance of a contract. Chapter 8 on bribery provides the variations of the schemes.

- **Progress payment fraud.** A contractor applies for payment during the course of a contract and fraudulently certifies that costs eligible for reimbursement have been incurred at a pace faster than actually incurred.

- **Nonconforming material or services.** A contractor provides materials or services that do not conform to the contract requirements. The schemes are product substitution, false reports, or nonconforming finished products.

- **Cost mischarging.** The contract is charged for costs not allowable under the contract or for costs relating to a separate contract. Secondly, the contract is falsely charged via the schemes described in Chapter 6.

For example, in a fixed price expenditure contract, the costs are fixed and the deliverable is defined in the contract. Determining the probable fraud scenario given the inherent fraud schemes follows:

- **A Defective pricing** scheme would apply if contract costs were intentionally understated for the sole purpose of winning the contact. The intent was to increase the costs through change orders, or the original cost was overstated via the techniques described in Chapter 8. Then, the contractor bills the agreed-on costs using a variation of an overbilling scheme.

- **A Progress payment** scheme would not apply because our contract calls for one payment at the completion of the contract.

- **A Cost mischarging** scheme would not apply because the costs are fixed. However if an actual cost change order were issued cost mischarging would apply.

- **A Nonconforming goods or services** scheme would apply because the only option available to the contractor would be product substitution.

Fraud Schemes for Mischarging

The basis for calculating and charging a contract creates predictable ways for contractors to fraudulently charge a contract. The first step for auditors is to determine whether the contract was overcharged. The second step is to determine whether the contractor intentionally concealed the true nature of the charges. The next sections discuss strategies for mischarging.

Intentional Errors Scheme   In the intentional errors scheme, the contractor inserts errors that would appear to be clerical or computational. If the errors are detected, the explanation is that the overcharges were an honest error. The fraudulent intent would be established through a consistent pattern of errors, a frequency of errors, or through an admission.

Audit Strategy:
1. Verify the arithmetic accuracy of all computations.
2. Compare charges to original supporting documents.
3. Compare supporting schedules to applicable accounting journals.
4. Review charges to determine charges are allowable and properly allocated.

False or Fictitious Charges Scheme   In the false or fictitious charges scheme, the expenditure did not occur or was never incurred by the contractor. The charges are supported by false documentation or the contractor states the documentation is missing. Fraudulent intent would be established by the fictitious nature of the charge.

Audit Strategy:

1. Examine original documents for signs of alteration.

2. Examine original documents for signs of creation. Consider confirming the charge with the stated vendor on the invoice.

3. Perform audit procedures for fictitious vendors.

4. Use independent sources to verify the deliverable of the item or service.

Overstated Actual Charge Scheme   In the overstated actual charge scheme, the documentation supporting the actual charge has been altered or created to support the overcharge. The act of altering or creating would establish the fraudulent intent. The overbilling schemes in collusion with a vendor identified in Chapter 6 would also apply.

Audit Strategy:

1. Examine original documents for signs of alteration or creation.

2. Perform overbilling audit procedures.

3. Use independent sources to verify the deliverable of the item or service.

Actual Charge Unrelated to the Contract Scheme   In the actual charge unrelated to the contract scheme, the charge could relate to the contract, but in fact provides no benefit to the contract. The false explanations or false documentation would establish the fraudulent intent. The next example illustrates the audit strategy involving payroll and supplies.

Audit Strategy:

1. **Payroll charges.** Examine time records to determine who originated the coding of the payroll charge to the specific contract. When the contract coding occurs by someone other than the employee, the likelihood of misallocation increases.

2. **Payroll charges.** Examine the personnel file and determine that the individual has the required qualifications for the job rating.

3. **Payroll charges.** Interview employees charged to the contract to determine their recollection of which contracts they worked on.

Ask the employee to bring calendars to the interview. Also confirm the individual's qualifications and resume history.

4. Confirm time and attendance through independent databases, building access, computer access, and parking lot access.

5. **Supplies charges.** Perform a logic analysis on the quantity of the items used on the contract.

Same Expenditure Charged to Multiple Contracts Scheme   In the same expenditure charged to multiple contracts scheme, the charge is for something related to the contract but not incurred. Since the charge is an actual expenditure, the documentation supporting the charge would be the original document. To avoid the likelihood of detection, the charge would most likely be made to various unrelated contracts. The multiple charging would establish the fraudulent intent.

Audit Strategy:
1. Identify all contracts under the control of a company or project manager over a time period. Determine how costs are allocated between the contracts. Based on the contract identification and the allocation methodology, select contracts for review of multiple charging.

2. Examine original documents noting vendor descriptions that are inconsistent with the nature of the contract, such as purchase order number, vendor shipping location, delivery location, contact person, sales tax calculation, or some other notation that may appear on the invoice.

3. Examine other contracts for evidence of the same expenditure. When the billing is supported by manually prepared schedules rather than accounting journals, the likelihood of the scheme occurring increases.

4. Confirm use of the item or services with employees working on the contract.

Prior Purchases Charged at Current Fair Market Value Scheme   In this scheme, the contractor has an inventory of items that were purchased prior to the contract at a lower unit rate. The contract is charged the current fair market rate rather than the original cost. Since the contract uses the word "cost," the fraudulent intent would be established by the act of charging the contract at a higher rate than incurred by the contractor.

Audit Strategy:
1. Examine shipping documents or bills of lading to determine the vendor receipt date.

2. Determine cost at time of receipt.

3. Determine if items were carried in inventory. Ascertain the original carry cost.

Increased Rates Solely for the Contract Scheme   The scheme of using increased rates solely for the contract, typically relates to payroll or payroll-related expenses. In this scheme, the employee or contractor rate is increased for the duration of the contract or for just one contract. This technique is applicable when the contractor receives a percentage fee based on direct expenses. The fraudulent intent is established by the changing of the rate for the one contract without cause.

Audit Strategy:
1. Examine the personnel file for evidence of rate or classification changes.

2. Examine employee W-2s before, during, and after the contract.

False Allocation of Charges Scheme   The false allocation of charges scheme has a number of variations that depend on the nature of the contract and how costs are applied. Schemes can include over allocating the cost of an invoice that relates to multiple contracts, depreciating fixed assets at a rate faster than the useful life, and service centers including costs that are already included in the overhead rate or in the direct costs. When the charge is posted from an original accounting journal, the fraudulent intent in these schemes is difficult to establish without an admission of guilt. The act of transferring the costs via journal entry tends to illustrate the intent.

Audit Strategy:
1. Search for journal entries transferring charges. Request documentation supporting the journal and verify the explanation.

2. Obtain documentation supporting how recharge costs rates were calculated. Verify the rate calculation.

Layering the Transaction Scheme   In a layering the transaction scheme, the false or overstated expenditure is incurred at the subcontract level. Then, the subcontractor passes through the overstated charge to the prime contractor. The technique used at the subcontract level conceals the fraud when the contract does not include a right to audit clause. The overbilling provides the prime contractor with a credit toward other unrelated contracts or a kickback. The fraudulent intent is established by the mere act of the layered transaction, the intentional overbilling, and the resulting kickback payment.

Audit Strategy:
1. Confirm costs through independent sources. For example, in a payroll charge, compare the charged rate to union rates.

2. Search for vendor refunds in the cash receipts journal.

3. If the contract has a right to audit clause at the subcontractor level, examine documentation supporting subcontract charges. Without a right to audit clause, ask to examine the subcontractor's records. The answer will be either yes or no.

Related Parties Scheme   In the related party's scheme, the parties intentionally overcharge each other to inflate the cost of the contract. The scheme is similar to the layered transaction scheme. The sheer nature of the related party transaction should be a red flag for the auditor.

Audit Strategy:
1. Determine whether related parties exist in the contract by reading the vendors' financial statements or performing background checks on vendors.

2. Determine the reasonableness of the expenditure through independent sources.

3. Request confirmation of whether the charges included a profit element. Even though the contractor may misrepresent the truth, the contractor's statement will provide evidence of intent at a later time.

Refunds or Rebates Not Applied to the Contract Scheme   In the scheme in which refunds or rebates are not applied, the contract is charged at gross or list price. The contractor actually pays the gross rate, and does not apply the subsequent credit to the contract.

Audit Strategy:
1. Assuming the vendor used by the contractor is not a party to the scheme, ask the vendor about rebates or refunds to the contractor.

2. Confirm pricing with the vendor through an interview pretext call regarding pricing for items in the contract.

False Contract Interpretation Scheme   The interpretation of contract wording or the lack of contract wording often facilitates false interpretation schemes. Assume the contract states that the charges are billed at cost. In the simplest of terms, cost would be defined as the amount paid for an item or service. What about a charge incurred through a company that is totally owned by the contractor? Is cost the amount paid, or is cost the amount paid less the profit earned by the contractor-owned company? If the second interpretation is correct, how would the profit be determined? False contract interpretation, by its nature, is an easy way to conceal a fraudulent overcharge. Therefore, establishing the fraudulent intent of the interpretation is difficult.

Audit Strategy:
1. Compare the contract language in prior or later contracts for obvious differences or interpretations.

2. Discuss contract terms with legal counsel to ascertain their interpretation of the contract.

3. Discuss contract terms with industry experts as to standard industry practices.

Expenditure Provides No Benefit to the Contract Scheme   In schemes involving expenditures that provide no benefit to the contract, the expenditure was not necessary or excessive, the item purchased was not used in the support of the contract, or equipment was used for an unrelated purpose. As an example, the contract anticipated the need for office equipment. The equipment item was purchased, but used for administrative purposes. Expenditures at the end of the contract should receive a closer scrutiny by auditors.

Audit Strategy:
1. **Equipment purchases.** Inspect the equipment as to location and use.

2. **Supply purchases at the end of the contract.** Determine whether the use of the quantity purchases was feasible within the time period.

3. Discuss necessity of the charge with company contract managers.

Overbilling Schemes in Contracts

Overbilling schemes in contracts occur in predictable ways. In reviewing contract charges, auditors need to be aware and plan for fraudulent charges. This checklist provides a list of the most common schemes in labor, material, and equipment.

Labor Rates Schemes:
- Fictitious employee
- Fictitious payroll reports
- Charging for no-show employees
- Overstated labor hours or rate

- Fictitious or altered time cards
- Inflating the job position and the corresponding rate
- Charging at a higher rate than the individual who performed the function
- Charging a level of effort that is not consistent with the actual effort
- Increasing employee rate for the contract
- Charging for non-allowable services or duties
- Charging for individuals already included in overhead rates
- Charging for contractor errors, mismanagement, or turnover
- Duplicate billing of employees
- Excessive charging of employees

Direct Material Schemes:
- Fictitious material and supplies
- Overstated material cost or rate
- Overstated quantity
- Provide substandard product
- Provide rebuilt or used products as new products
- Provide nonspecification product
- Provide counterfeit products
- Provide equivalent products
- Failure to test product as required
- Provide false certifications as to the quality or specifications
- Duplicate billing of the same material
- Charging for materials previously purchased and charged at today's prices
- No credit for returns, adjustments, rebates, allowances, or warranty issues
- Conspiracy between contractor and supplier to overcharge
- Conspiracy between contractor and subcontractor to overcharge
- Related party profits on materials charged to contract
- Contractor does not perform fiduciary responsibility to obtain fair and reasonable pricing

- Charging for contractor errors, mismanagement, or turnover
- Equipment Rental Schemes
- Fictitious equipment
- Overstated rate of equipment
- Overstated hours of usage
- Charged for higher rate equipment than provided
- Charged for equipment idle at site
- Charged for higher-rate equipment than needed

8

Bribery

Unfortunately, corruption is a cost of doing business. We can debate the moral implications of the statement; we can focus on the various worldwide initiatives to curb corruption. Nevertheless, corruption is a cost of doing business. The question from an audit perspective is whether auditors prevent, detect, or deter corrupt business practices. For reasons to be discussed in the chapter, it is the detection of corrupt business practices by auditors that corresponds to the purpose of this book. Although, the same type of fraud risks exist in the revenue cycle, the focus of the chapter is on fraud in the procurement process, specifically, bribery.

Clearly, bribery is illegal, whether committed in a public or a commercial environment. Therefore, from a legal perspective, there are various forms of corrupt acts, differentiated as either criminal or civil. In performing an investigation, statutes provide the basis for the legal action. However, the burden of proof becomes overbearing from an audit perspective because the elements of the various laws generally cannot be directly applied in performing an audit.

Auditors need to understand that laws focus on acts committed by the parties under the law. Therefore, they should look to the law to determine what acts are observable within the course of the audit or the red flags of a fraudulent act. Auditors should use the corrupt acts as the basis for conducting the audit, while understanding the limitations of proving the act within the confines of the audit process.

UNDERSTANDING THE LEGAL TERMS

Even though there are limitations of proving corrupt acts within the audit process, auditors still must understand the corrupt acts in legal terms.

Legal sources are necessary for this understanding. For the scope of this book, the legal terms used are from *Black's Law Dictionary*. Some of the relevant definitions are:

> **Bribery.** A price, reward, gift, or favor bestowed or promised with a view to pervert the judgment of or influence the action of a person in a position of trust.
>
> **Commercial Bribery.** A supposedly disinterested appraiser's acceptance of a benefit that influences the appraisal of the goods or services.
>
> **Corruption.** The act of doing something with an intent to give some advantage inconsistent with official duty and the rights of others; a fiduciary's or official's use of a station or office to procure some benefit either personally or for someone else, contrary to the rights of others.
>
> **Gratuity.** Done or performed without obligation to do so; given without consideration in circumstances that do not otherwise impose a duty.
>
> **Extortion.** The act or practice of obtaining something or compelling some action by illegal means, as by force or coercion.
>
> **Kickback.** A return of a portion of a monetary sum received, especially because of coercion or a secret agreement.
>
> **Conflict of Interest.** A real or seeming incompatibility between one's private interests and one's public or fiduciary duties.

Statutes

It is important for auditors to understand the legal perspective regarding the required elements of proof. *The Federal Bribery and Gratuity Statute* provides such an understanding.

The Federal Bribery and Gratuity Statute includes two separate crimes: bribery of public officials and illegal gratuity given to public officials. "The statute seeks to punish both public officials who accept bribes or illegal gratuities, as well as those who intend to influence public officials with such benefits."[1] The four relevant questions to ask when presented with a federal bribery case are:

1. Is the official a current or future "public official" under the statute?

2. Was the benefit given, offered, or promised to the "public official," or was it demanded, sought, received, or accepted by the "public official"?

---

[1]*White Collar Crime*, 2nd ed. (West Group, 2002), chapter 49, section 49-2.

3. Was the benefit a "thing of value" under the statute?

4. Was the gift, offer, or promise made with corrupt intent or intent to influence an official act?

In addition to bribery of public officials, auditors must understand commercial bribery. Specifically, in commercial bribery, a vendor offers money or gifts to the employee for influencing purchasing decisions without the consent of the employer and contrary to the best interests of the employer.

Audit Definitions versus Legal Definitions

In a legal context, a "favored party" is the process of providing one party with a concealed advantage over the other parties. The "intent of the advantage" is to corruptly influence the decision process toward one party to the detriment of the awarding organization and to the advantage of the individual corrupting the process, or the vendor or customer receiving the corrupt advantage. The awarding manager is influenced by a bribe or kickback and awards the contract to the vendor. When addressing a case of bribery, the auditor must understand the legal definitions of bribery, "favored party" and "intent of the advantage." Once understood, the auditor proceeds to establish the key elements for a bribery case from an audit perspective, in essence, developing the audit definition. The key elements of establishing a bribery case from an audit perspective are:

- **Parties to the Contract.** The parties are either directly or indirectly involved with the contract.

- **Without Consent of the Organization.** The organization's policies and procedures for awarding a contract are clear. The parties acted outside these policies and procedures.

- **Influencing the Contract.** The parties intended to corruptly influence any official act or decision in awarding or accepting the contract.

- **Where and How Influence Occurs.** The undue reward did in fact influence the behavior of a public official or manager.

- **With Knowledge.** The company manager acted contrary to the known rules of honesty and integrity.

- **Received Something of Value.** The company manager receives an undue reward.

- **Item of Value was Intended to Corrupt the Decision Process.** The contractor corruptly gives, offers, or promises anything of value.

In addition, favored vendor schemes can occur after a vendor is legitimately awarded the contract. Examples include: the purchasing manager seeks to receive a kickback from the vendor; the vendor offers a kickback to the purchasing manager; or the purchasing manager provides a corrupt preferential treatment that allows the vendor to effectively inflate the contract cost or accept nonconforming goods or services. The audit definition developed by the auditors for procurement schemes is easily tailored to bank loans, sales contracts, security sales, or trades of any kind.

AUDIT ELEMENTS

The key elements in establishing a case for bribery from an audit perspective were listed above to illustrate the relationship between the legal definitions applying to such a case and the corresponding audit definitions. Although auditors need to understand the legal basis of corrupt acts, such as bribery, the following key elements provide the necessary audit basis.

Parties to the Contract

Auditors must identify the internal party who awarded the contract and the internal party who influenced the award. The audit should document the recipient of the contract.

Without Consent of the Organization

Auditors should determine the organization's policies and procedures for awarding a contract. The first question is: Did the employee operate in a manner inconsistent with policies or procedures? Employees also have an obligation to operate in the best interest of the company. Legal counsel can advise auditors on breach of fiduciary responsibility legal theories.

Influencing the Contract

The audit process should focus on influence and favoritism by identifying evidence of influence or favoritism in the process, false documentation or false representations, correlating communication mediums with awarding contracts, or evidence of the bribe tax. Influence occurs in three ways:

1. **Overt.** Directly impacts purchase process or documentation. The typical audit process is designed to examine for overt red flags within the:

   - Request for proposal (RFP)
   - Bid responses from vendor
   - Other correspondence in the bid file
   - Bid process

○   Criteria for selection

○   Selection decision

2. **Covert.** Provide or conceal information to the advantage of one vendor. The typical audit process is not designed to search for covert techniques. Therefore, the audit process would need to be changed to include such procedures or incorporate the techniques into the investigation plan. The result of the examination would be a suspicious pattern of coincidence surrounding purchase issuance and the dates and times of the communication between the employee and vendor. Typical sources of information would be:

○   Appointment calendar

○   Visitors log

○   Security logs

○   Telephone: land and cell

○   Fax logs

○   E-mail

○   Express mail services

○   Travel

○   Correspondence files

○   Observation

○   Witness statement

3. **Indirect influence.** Uses management position or personal integrity to influence others to award purchase to vendor. Typically, there is no documentation of the indirect influence. The audit examination would learn of these activities through interviews. The result would be to show that the employee viewed the suggestion as a directive because of past events.

With Knowledge

A key element of an audit is to prove that the bribe in fact corruptly influenced the manager's decision to award the contract. The mere acceptance of a gift from a vendor may not be sufficient to rise to the standard of influence. However, if the company has a policy specifically prohibiting gift acceptance and the employee had or should have knowledge of the policy, the violation maybe sufficient to establish the knowledge requirement. Auditors should work closely with legal counsel regarding this matter.

The second part of "with knowledge" is to show that the company manager knew that the representation was false, not an honest error. Illustrating the knowledge factor is a critical aspect of the audit process.

Where and How Influence Occurs

A method needs to be established to assess where and how influencing the awarding of a contract occurs. The use of a structured methodology to assess the fraud risk facilitates the planning phase of the audit. The typical schemes for influencing the contract are:

- Avoiding the bid process through false representations
- Providing false responses to the RFP
- Providing advance communication of information to one vendor
- Management override by deviating from established procedures
- Using control opportunity to create favored conditions for one vendor

Received Something of Value

The bribe or kickback is a cost of doing business in a corrupt environment. The payment of the bribe or the kickback requires a method of factoring the bribe tax into the contract. If one were to develop a normal distribution curve using the costs of contracts, the bribe tax would increase the "norm" by between 5 and 15 percent. From an investigative rationale, bribes at the lower end of the scale tend to be tangible gifts; the higher bribes tend to be currency or cash equivalents.

Bribes can be paid directly or through layered or disguised payments. Once a bribe is identified, the investigation must show how the bribe corruptly influenced the decision process. Linking the receipt of the bribe to the influence is the last part of the investigation. This link is referred to as the *mens rea,* or the mental element. The investigator must show how the bribe influenced the awarding of the contract.

The purpose of such an investigation is to gather evidence to prove the elements of the applicable bribery or bribery-related statues. In a bribe or kickback scheme, auditors must investigate by examining the vendor's books or obtaining a confession from one of the parties. Typical ways of paying a bribe are:

- Prepaid credit cards or gift cards
- Employees on the payroll that are effectively no-show employees
- Trips or events

- False billing schemes via front companies (The company could be a way to convert checks to cash, or the internal employee is the beneficial owner of the front company.)

- Access to lease items, such as apartments, automobiles, boats

- Interest-free loans or loans incurred by the vendor with the proceeds going to the internal employee

Item of Value Was Intended to Corrupt the Decision Process

The competitive purchasing process is intended to ensure that contracts are awarded to vendors at the right price, quality, and quantity. The bidding process is intended to provide documentation that the process occurred in accordance with policies and procedures.

Purchasing fraud or defective pricing is intended to corrupt the process to ensure one particular vendor receives the contract. The awarding of the contract is to the detriment of the organization. The internal party awarding the contract is looking for a bribe or a kickback. Since the reward aspect of the corruption process is an off-the-book transaction, typically the actual proof is gathered during the investigative process, not the audit process.

AUDIT OBJECTIVES

The purpose of the audit is to ensure compliance with stated procedures or laws and to be on the lookout for the red flags of fraud. Therefore, the reasonable expectation of the audit process is to identify a vendor that received a concealed favored status within the selection process. The bribe by its nature is an off-the-book transaction for the audit process. Because the bribe cannot be directly observed in the audit process, auditors must identify contracts that should be investigated for bribery, extortion, or vendor bid rigging. The six audit objectives for favored vendor status include determining:

1. How the parties corruptly influenced the purchasing process

2. That the representation regarding the process, assumptions, documentation, qualifications, requirements, or the management decision is false

3. That the parties making the representation knew or had knowledge or should have had knowledge that the representation was false

4. The technique to inflate the costs to fund the bribe tax

5. The damages to the company due to the corrupt awarding of the contract

6. Through an investigative process that the purchasing manager received a bribe for influencing the awarding of the contract or a kickback through the administration of the contract

Audit Objective One

"How the parties corruptly influenced the purchasing process."
The schemes used to corrupt the bid process provide the basis for defining the red flags of favoritism or the fraud theory for data mining. Understanding how each scheme or scheme variation operates will help in the awareness phase of fraud identification. The scheme can also function as a red flag to identify vendor relationships that have the characteristics of a corrupt relationship. The data mining can search for the specific fraud scheme variation. The approach used will depend on the philosophy of the auditor and the reason for the audit.

The starting point is to identify one transaction that meets the definition of the scheme. The second step is to search for a pattern of favoritism by vendor or by purchasing agent through the use of the noted scheme or through the use of other schemes. The pattern of activity becomes the key to the audit process to show the intent of the purchasing decision process. Once the pattern is identified, auditors should identify the facts that exist to show that the purchasing agents had knowledge of the favoritism.

These schemes are used to corrupt the competitive purchasing process:

- Bid avoidance
- False statements
- Advance communication of information
- Management override
- Favoring of key control points
- Vendor bid rigging

Bid Avoidance   Bid avoidance consists of structuring the procurement process to circumvent or avoid the bidding requirements. The typical schemes to avoid the bid process are:

- **Aggregate purchasing.** This is the process of issuing multiple purchase orders to the same vendor or a related vendor. Each purchase order is below the bid threshold level. However, in aggregate, the purchase orders exceed the bid threshold. The key is to show that the parties had knowledge of the true purchase requirements.

- **Split bids.** This is the process of awarding two vendors a purchase order for the same product. The key is to show that the organization received no benefit from splitting the contract.

- **Contract extension.** Contract extension is the process of awarding the vendor additional work assignments without following the competitive bid process. The red flag would be an approval for additional work assignments.

- **Sole source.** The process requires showing that the sole-source statement was false. The second step is to show the manager had or should have had knowledge that the statement was false.

- **Emergency purchases.** The process requires showing that the emergency condition did not exist or that the manager intentionally waited for the emergency to occur. An emergency condition is often used as a reason to bypass normal controls. Auditors should look for kickback schemes that may be occurring due to bypassing of the bidding process. If the emergency condition is genuine, the question becomes whether the right vendor was selected as to price and quality. In this case, auditors will need to conduct vendor surveys regarding price and quality.

- **No attempt to obtain bids.** The reasons no attempts to obtain bids were made are not documented and are supported solely by oral explanations.

- **Management override.** Here management directs the purchase to a specific vendor without a bidding process. The manager representations are typically false in total or part.

False Statements   Here the bid file contains false documents or the non-disclosure of conflicts-of-interest. The typical false statement schemes follow.

- **Fictitious bids are submitted** from a fictitious company or using a real company's name. The purchasing agent prepares the bid. Auditors should examine the bids for a degree of coincidence (i.e., the same paper type, format, or errors) and should consider confirming the bids with the noted companies.

- **Real companies knowingly submit false bids.** The vendor has been told they would not receive the contract, but would be considered for future contracts.

- **False vendor qualifications are supplied.** The vendor's work experience as stated has not occurred.

- **Disorganized files or massive unnecessary files** hinder auditors' analysis of the bids.

- **False evaluation of the vendors' bids.** The false evaluation typically involves qualitative aspects of the bid process regarding product delivery and product reliability.

- **Undisclosed conflicts-of-interest or hidden ownership.** A company employee may have undisclosed ownership in the vendor.

Advance Communication of Information   The purchasing manager provides information to one vendor to the detriment of other vendors. The typical schemes in the advance communication schemes are:

- **Advance information.** The vendor has knowledge of the request for proposal before other vendors.

- **Discrepancy between bid projections and actual purchases.** Typically, the scheme occurs by purchasing a greater quantity or a different quality than the RFP states.

- **Information regarding future changes.** The scheme allows a vendor to bid lower than the competition due to knowledge of specific change orders.

Consider this example. The RFP states that the vendor will purchase 1,000 widgets. However, the true intent of the manager is to purchase 10,000 widgets. Let us further assume this information regarding fair market value:

- At 1,000 purchased, the unit cost per widget is $10.00.

- At 10,000 purchased, the unit cost per widget is $9.00.

The favored vendor who has advance information can underbid others. In this example, the favored vendor bids $9.50 per widget and receives the contract. Although the bid file indicates that the lowest-price vendor was selected, the company paid $5,000 more than necessary.

Management Override   In this scheme, the purchasing agent deviates from bidding procedures to benefit a specific vendor. The typical methods are:

- **Deviations from bidding procedures**
  - Accepting late bids
  - Resubmitting or changing bids

- ○ Negotiating after the opening of bids
- ○ Changing requirements after the opening of bids
- **Limited time allowed for bidding, with advance communication with one specific vendor**
  - ○ Decreasing the time allowed to respond to a bid
  - ○ Bid time occurs during significant holidays
  - ○ Publishing the bid notice in a newspaper with limited distribution
- **Communication of bid information**
  - ○ Inconsistencies with bidders' conference
  - ○ Sole-source communication of bidders' information

Favoring of Key Control Points
- Establishing a need
- Specification setting/communication of information
- Identifying the vendor pool
- Establishing the selection criteria/bid evaluation/vendor selection

Establishing a Need   In real estate, the old adage is that location, location, and location established the fair market value. The same is true for purchasing items. If an item is procured at peak times, logic dictates that the price will be higher. The margin earned by the vendor also is higher. Techniques used to intentionally inflate contract prices follow.

- **Purchasing items intentionally at peak demand times for item.** Typically, the pricing at peak times results in paying list price, which results in the largest margin for the vendor. Auditors need to establish when managers identified their needs and the causes for the delay in procuring the item.

- **Purchasing under emergency conditions bypass all logical controls.** If a shortage of a critical item occurs, then purchasing controls may be suspended to obtain the item on a timely basis.

Specification Setting/Communication of Information   In a purchase specifications scheme, the bid influence occurs through the design of the specifications in a manner to ensure that only one vendor can be awarded the contract. Auditors should be alert to these red flags:

- **Vagueness or lack of clarity in specifications.** This vagueness allows the vendor to bid in a manner that seems cost effective when in fact the pricing is higher than that of other vendors. Assume the specifications call for a price per case. The industry standard is 48 units per case; however, the selected vendor is providing 24 units per case. The lack of clarity on the quantity per case allows the false awarding of the purchase order. Auditors should determine industry standards for communicating specifications on quantity, quality, or product description or confirm the exact number provided.

- **Restrictive specifications favor the pre-selected vendor.** Auditors should compare the selected vendor's sales literature to the RFP. If the RFP has a high degree of similarity to the vendor's sales catalog, it is likely that the bid was structured to favor the vendor.

- **Prequalification strategies.** Where prequalification strategies exist unnecessary vendor requirements restrict the choice of vendors

- **Criteria are established to favor the selected vendor.** With advance communication, the vendor can respond in a manner to maximize the existing criteria. Auditors should determine if the criteria are valid or created to favor the vendor.

- **Vendor criteria established after the bid opening.** Auditors should establish when the vendor criteria were established.

- **RFPs contain intentional defects.** Here the favored vendor is aware of the RFP's intentional defects.

- **Vendor prepares specifications.** The vendor establishes the RFP and then bids on the contract.

- **After the fact, financial adjustments due to specifications.** Here the selected vendor has prior knowledge of the financial adjustments that will occur, which allows the vendor to bid unreasonably low.

Identifying the Vendor Pool   One of the keys to ensuring competitive purchasing is to identify vendors that are ready, willing, and able to offer competitive prices. An easy way to corrupt the process is to exclude qualified vendors or limit the vendor pool. Examples of schemes to exclude qualified vendors follow.

- **Excluding qualified vendors by not including them on the bidders' list.** Auditors should search for other qualified vendors through trade associations, yellow pages, Web searches, or discussions with other subsidiaries or audit departments in similar industries. The use of Web postings for RFPs is an effective control to minimize the risk.

- **Failure to mail or distribute RFPs as stated in the bid file.** Auditors should confirm that all vendors on the list received the RFP. The use of Web-based postings of RFPs minimizes the risk of the scheme.

- **Providing vendors with false or misleading RFPs to discourage them from bidding.** Auditors should confirm with all the vendors on the list that they received the same RFP.

- **Limiting the search for qualifying vendors.** The process places arbitrary limits on the geographic boundaries on the vendor search. Auditors should corroborate the business need for the limits established.

- **Dissimilar vendors to provide illusion of search.** The vendor name, Standard Industrial Classification code, or company description indicates that the vendor is a comparable source when in fact its business structure is not consistent with the true need of the company.

- **Withdrawal of bidders.** This is a red flag, especially if the bidder becomes a subcontractor.

Establishing the Selection Criteria/Bid Evaluation/Vendor Selection   The vendor selection process is the final step of the bidding process. These schemes are used to favor a vendor while providing the illusion of a fair and open selection process:

- **Vendor bypasses normal review process.**

- **Communicating other vendors' pricing information to the favored vendor.** Pricing information should never be disclosed unless the terms of the RFP indicate that a price negotiation phase will follow the submission phase. If price disclosure occurs, auditors should determine that all vendors had an equal opportunity to reconsider their pricing based on the competition's pricing. In reality, the practice encourages vendors to submit higher prices on the original quote.

- **Lost bids or information.** The purchasing agent destroys a vendor's submission of a bid. Auditors should contact vendors on the RFP that did not submit a bid and confirm the fact. It is also a good idea to ask why the vendor did not submit a bid.

- **False calculations of vendors' cost.** Cost calculations are not as simple as one unit price times a quantity. In those instances where multiple price considerations exist, auditors should recompute the anticipated costs.

- **Vendor selection criteria favors a specific vendor.** Schemes involve:

  ○ Creating criteria after bid opening

  ○ Changing criteria after bid opening

  ○ Scoring system favors a specific vendor

  ○ False statements regarding vendor assessment

From a control perspective, the criteria for evaluating vendors must be stated before the opening of bid files. The criteria must be consistent with actual business needs. The operating department should establish the criteria, and purchasing should be able to challenge the criteria on economic purchase grounds. In reality, assessing vendor selection criteria is difficult and subjective. Auditors should ensure that the criteria for vendor selection are established and consistent with company objectives.

The red flags of these schemes may also be indicative of favored vendor status due to internal management decisions. (See Exhibit 8.1.)

Vendor Bid Rigging   Vendor bid rigging by definition is a fraud scheme perpetrated by vendors. Internal management does not have knowledge or does not participate in the fraud scheme. The vendors agree among themselves as to who will win the contract.

The typical methods for vendors in bid-rigging schemes are:

- **Intentional unresponsive bids.** These bids provide the impression of competitive bidding but, in reality, suppliers agree to submit bids at a certain cost to ensure that the predetermined vendor is awarded the contract. The red flags are the bid price exceeding the original estimates or the amount of difference between the award cost and next highest bid price.

- **Bid suppression.** Bid suppression is an agreement among suppliers either to abstain from bidding or to withdraw bids. The red flags are limited responses, bidders that normally bid on the contract do not submit a bid, or when a supplier that either did not participate or withdrew its bid becomes a subcontractor.

- **Bid rotation.** In the bid rotation process, the pre-selected supplier submits the lowest bid on a systematic or rotating basis. The red flag is the pattern of awards to vendors over an extended time.

- **Market division.** This scheme is an arrangement among suppliers not to compete in designated geographic regions or for specific customers. The red flag is the fact that a qualified vendor is unwillingly to submit a bid.

Audit Objective Two

"That the representation regarding the process, assumptions, documentation, qualifications, requirements, or the management decision is false."

The falsity of the representation becomes the key to attacking the creditability of the operating manager. The easiest way to determine falsity is through an admission by the manager. Other approaches include gathering documents, either internal or external to the organization, that refute the

Exhibit 8.1   Red Flags of Bid Documentation Matrix

Company Name
Matrix Red Flags Theory
Risk Unit: Red Flags of Bid Documentation

Type of Red Flag	Request for Proposal	Bid	Vendor Identification	Vendor Award	Other
Anomaly	All information communicated verbally	Commonality of vendor bids	Sole source	Highest-priced vendor selected	Bid canceled after opening
Vagueness	No list of vendors requested to submit bid	Quantity and quality description	No physical address identified for vendors	Criteria for selection not clearly defined	Unclear as to ownership
Restrictive	Identifies specific brand and model	Limited time allowed for response	Time, delivery, and location limitations	Other vendors excluded based on qualifications	All information through one individual
Missing	Unable to locate copy of RFP	Unable to locate copy of bids	Unable to locate list of vendors requested to submit bids	Bids not received from requested vendors	None
Illogical	Received three bids at same time	Rebid; Negotiate price after opening	Required vendor qualifications	Bid occurrences for same item in one year	Emergency status

Exhibit 8.1   Red Flags of Bid Documentation Matrix (*continued*)

Company Name
Matrix Red Flags Theory
Risk Unit: Red Flags of Bid Documentation

Type of Red Flag	Request for Proposal	Bid	Vendor Identification	Vendor Award	Other
Frequency	Same vendors requested each year	Same vendors bid each year	Same vendors requested each year	Last bid received wins award each year	Bid occurrences for same item in one year
Range	None	Vendor bid prices	Total capabilities and size of vendors	Projected cost	Dissimilar vendors
Change	Number of changes to original RFP specifications	Rebid; Allow changes to original bid	Vendors added to list after initial mailing	Change orders in close proximity to vendor award	Withdrawn vendor identified as subcontractor
Error	Disclosure of error to one vendor	Same error in vendors' bids	Excluding a qualified vendor	Rating and ranking vendor evaluation criteria	False representation regarding qualifications
Arithmetic	None	None	Error in calculating vendor evaluation score	Error in calculating total vendor costs	None
Unusual	Vendor assists in writing RFP	All bids exceed original estimates	Same vendors each year	Same vendor each year	Bypass bid process

representation, retrospective analysis of the contract administration, author-itative sources, or industry experts.

Audit Objective Three

"That the parties making the representation knew or had knowledge or should have had knowledge that the representation was false."
This step is typically the difficult part of establishing the intent to defraud the organization. However, the law requires the audit conclusions to demonstrate the difference between bad judgment and intent to cor-rupt the process. The intent factor can be established showing knowledge through prior contracts, pointing to training seminars or attendance at trade conferences, internal documents, or statements from other parties. Often the evidence is circumstantial, not direct. Auditors should consult with legal counsel to establish the burden of proof under this criteria.

Audit Objective Four

"The technique to inflate the costs to fund the bribe tax."
The more common ways to factor the bribe tax into the contract are:

- **Inflating the total cost of the contract** at the award time or changing orders with inflated costs.

- **Making after-the-fact price adjustments.** The scheme typically occurs in tangible items that have normal price fluctuations due to market conditions. The scheme operates best in an environment with large quantity volumes because a price difference of a penny can cause a sufficient overbilling situation.

- **Provide for product substitution, billing for a higher cost item than delivered.** The technique is typically used in supply items that are consumed on a daily basis or items for which the average person would be unable to differentiate between the ordered item and the delivered item.

- **False billing, billing for products or services not provided.** The technique is more typical in services due to the difficulty in determin-ing the exact number of hours dedicated to a project.

Audit Objective Five

"The damages to the company due to the corrupt awarding of the contract."
The damages consist of the difference between the cost paid and the fair market price in an arm's-length transaction. In establishing the arm's-length price, auditors need to establish assumptions that are supported by authoritative sources. Professional trade organizations or industry experts

are useful sources to identify fair market pricing. The report should clearly identify the method of computation and cite the sources.

Audit Objective Six

"Through an investigative process the purchasing manager received a bribe for influencing the awarding of the contract or a kickback through the administration of the contract."

One approach is to obtain a statement from the vendor that it in fact provided a bribe or kickback. This technique requires auditors to confront the vendor and request assistance.

The second approach is to request the right to examine the vendor's books for evidence of a bribe. The request has two possible answers: yes or no. Auditors should make this request only when they have sufficient evidence to believe that a corrupt situation exists. The decision must be supported by management.

The fact that the vendor is willing to open its books is a good sign or a sign that the vendor knows that the bribe occurred in an off-the-books transaction. If the vendor refuses the audit request, management needs to decide whether to continue doing business with the vendor.

9

Travel Expenses

Many auditors have stopped auditing travel expenses because of the materiality of the expense. While there is no argument that an individual expense report is not material or that total travel expenses are not material to the company, there are other reasons to audit travel expenses. Primarily, it seems that fraud investigations involving management usually include travel expenses. Consequently, travel expense fraud by management may be an excellent and inexpensive fraud risk assessment procedure. The logic being: if managers are committing travel fraud, then what other frauds are they committing? In addition, many fraud auditors have indicated that frauds start small and grow. To prevent such growth, catching or discouraging an individual from committing travel fraud may act as a fraud deterrent. Lastly, the audit of travel expenses works as an integrity barometer of the organization.

The Rationale for Travel Expense Fraud

The rationale for travel fraud includes: the intent to cover nonreimbursable expenses, to disguise inappropriate customer entertainment, a sense of entitlement, to conceal individual expenses considered too high for reimbursement, or to receive reimbursement for actual expenses where the original receipt was lost. However, travel reimbursement, customs, practices, and policies vary by company. The acceptability of an expense in one company would be inappropriate in another company. Auditors must understand what is normal and customary under the company's travel reimbursement practices.

Travel expense abuse consists of submitting an expense that is not consistent with the company's polices and practices. The abuse is associated with the amount, nature, or frequency of the expense reimbursement.

Typically, the employee does not view the reimbursement as inappropriate, but rather the reimbursement policy as too restrictive. The abuse is concealed in the same manner as the travel fraud or by circumventing the approval process.

Travel Expense Concealment Strategies

Travel fraud results in the employee obtaining reimbursement for expenses that did not occur, duplicate reimbursement, higher reimbursement than the actual expense, unauthorized expenses and bribes to customers. The fraud is concealed through a falsely stated business purpose, improper expense characterization, or false receipts. The concealment can be categorized in these ways:

- "Travel characterization" is describing the expense in a false manner. For example, entertainment expenses are described as a business meal. Business lunches are submitted as overnight travel expenses. Personal expenses are described as business.

- "No business purpose" is falsely describing the business purpose of the expense or trip. By tax law, travel and entertainment expenses require a business purpose for the expense. The employee provides a false description of the business purpose. For example, when the traveler takes a friend to dinner but describes the expense as a business meeting.

- "Falsification of receipts" is the process of altering a receipt, creating a receipt, or colluding with a vendor to obtain a false receipt.

Who Commits Travel Expense Fraud

Auditors should establish criteria for selecting expense reports and use block sampling to focus on a number of reports for a specific traveler during a concentrated period. Using block sampling will allow auditors to spot trends and patterns of abuse. Employees in the following categories should be considered for travel expense account audits.

- Frequent travelers based on dollars and frequency
- Executive management
- Employees on the fast track
- Employees whose business travel standards are higher than personal travel standards
- Employees who normally incur entertainment expenses

- Departments with high direct-bill travel expenses
- Departments or employees with previously known problems

AUDIT EXAMINATION OF TRAVEL EXPENSES

As with most fraud schemes, the auditors need to apply the fraud theory to travel expenses. The red flags are specific to the type of travel expense fraud scheme.

The Red Flags of Travel Expense Fraud

During the examination of travel receipts, auditors need to be aware of the red flags of suspicious travel expenses. Auditors should look for these red flags in travel receipts:

- **Dates and times events occur.** As to the specific event or in relation to other events, e.g., the airport parking receipt indicates three days of parking expense, but the hotel indicates a five-day stay. Obviously there are viable explanations; however, initially the difference should be treated as a red flag.

- **Location.** Auditors must verify that the travel expense occurred in the city associated with the trip or company location.

- **Manual receipts versus credit card receipts.** Concerning manual receipts, auditors should note the handwriting style and signs of alteration. Alteration can be noted by looking for multiple blunt point ends and signs of lines having different thicknesses.

- **Method of payment is not consistent with known credit card numbers.** Auditors should ensure all credit card numbers on submitted credit card receipts match known employee credit card numbers.

- **Receipts missing information.** Credit card receipts typically indicate the name of the restaurant at the top of the receipt. In fraud, the traveler tears off the top portion to disguise the fact that the meal expense was incurred at a local restaurant.

- **Cash-based expenses versus credit card receipts.** Cash-based expenses are easier to disguise than credit card receipts. Auditors should note the handwriting style.

- **Consistency in reporting the business purpose or description of the event.** Travelers committing travel expense fraud tend to commit the same scheme on several expense reports.

- **Consistency in handwriting.** If the handwriting is similar on different receipts from different vendors, then the employee may have created the receipt.

Travel Expense Fraud Schemes

Airline Ticket Swapping Scheme   This fraud deals with reimbursement for a higher-price ticket than the actual ticket traveled. Historically, travelers would submit first-class travel ticket receipts, but would actually travel in coach. Then, they would pocket the difference between the first-class ticket price and the coach ticket. However, in today's world of multiple fare prices, the scheme could occur by submitting for a full-fare coach ticket, but traveling on a highly discounted airline. The red flags are the fare basis on the airline receipt. The higher the fare basis, the more likely the ticket could be part of a ticket swap scheme. Travelers may also purchase tickets with a higher fare basis to take advantage of frequent flyer programs. Remember though, this maybe a customary practice in a company.

Often vendors purchase a ticket for an employee to visit a plant location. In this fraud, the traveler will submit the vendor-purchased ticket for reimbursement. The scheme could also occur when the traveler is traveling for another organization. The red flag is when the method of payment on the airline receipt does not match known methods of payment for the traveler or the lack of normal airline receipts.

Direct Bill Arrangement Scheme   In the direct bill fraud, travelers submit a travel receipt with their expense report that is also billed to the company through the accounts payable process. Common areas for this scheme are hotel, car or limousine services, or all-inclusive travel events, when the traveler is on an extended business trip. The travel receipt may reference a purchase order number or some other company account number.

Travelers may also have multiple company credit cards. Procurement cards are a popular tool to eliminate small-dollar purchases from being processed through accounts payable. Travelers may charge the expense to their procurement cards, then submit a duplicate receipt with their expense reports.

Multiple Reimbursements Scheme   The multiple reimbursements scheme operates two different ways.

1. The employee is traveling for two different organizations. He or she requests reimbursement from both organizations for the same travel expense.

2. Employees are traveling together, and each one seeks reimbursement for the same expense. Cab fares and meals are a common area for this scheme.

Fictitious or Altered Receipts Scheme   Another fraud consists of travelers submitting receipts that have been altered or created to support a specific expense. Some things to watch for on receipts include:

Credit Card Receipts
- Is the restaurant name listed on the receipt?
- Is the date and time of meal on the receipt?
- Is the date and time of the receipt consistent with the characterization of the meal?
- Is the credit card number consistent with known credit card numbers of the traveler?
- Is the approval code on the receipt? False credit card receipts are often not credit checked.
- Is the meal amount consistent with the price range of meals at the restaurant?
- Is the receipt missing logical information?
- Is the receipt altered or changed as to date or amount?
- Is the receipt arithmetically correct? Intentional errors in totaling the receipt can result in credits on the traveler's credit card statement.

Manual Restaurant Receipts
- Is the restaurant name listed on the receipt?
- Is the receipt number in sequence with other receipts?
- Does the traveler normally charge or pay cash for meal expenses?
- Is the meal amount consistent with a cash-only restaurant or cash payment for a meal?
- Is the traveler traveling with other employees or vendors?
- Is the receipt missing logical information?
- Is the receipt altered or changed as to date or amount?
- Is the handwriting similar to that of the traveler?
- Is there consistency of ink on the various receipts?

Schemes Involving Disguised Local Expenses or Disguised Personal Trips   Disguised local expenses are concealed by removing or altering the name of the restaurant, and the date and time of the event, on the receipt.

The receipt is submitted as a travel expense, when in fact the expense was not incurred in travel status.

Disguised personal trips are hidden by falsely representing the nature of the trip. Typically, the length of the stay is not consistent with the stated business purpose. There is a difference between structuring a personal trip around a valid business trip and a business trip created for personal reasons. A red flag is triggered when the length of the stay is not consistent with the business trip, expenses are not included in the expense reimbursement, or knowledge of the traveler's personal life.

Supervisor Swap Scheme   In this scheme, the supervisor requires a subordinate to incur an expense that the supervisor knows the employer would not approve. The expense is for an amount higher than normally allowable, or not allowable due to the nature of the expense or the business location. The red flags are a higher-ranked employee in attendance or amounts or nature of the expense not typical for the traveler.

Internal Entertaining Scheme   The internal entertaining scheme is the process of characterizing an expense as a necessary or allowable one. Typically, the business purpose stated on the expense report is false. The pattern or frequency of the business meal or trip is the red flag to the abuse.

Cash Conversion Scheme   In the cash conversion scheme, the traveler obtains cash or a vendor gift receipt and submits a credit card receipt from the vendor supporting the expense. The expenditure would be represented as a meal expense or entertainment expense. Many restaurants now have shops at their location. The traveler purchases clothes, and then seeks reimbursement as a meal expense. A red flag would be an even amount on the credit card receipt or frequency of going to the same restaurant. The cash conversion scheme does not typically occur at chain restaurants. Unfortunately, there is no obvious red flag of the event. Some organizations now require a detailed receipt to be submitted with every credit card receipt. Auditors should understand if a restaurant owner is willing to provide cash to the traveler, they would most likely provide a false meal receipt as well.

Sex Shop Scheme   The names of many gentlemen's clubs sound like restaurants. The vendor code is a restaurant code rather than a nightclub. In these schemes, the traveler visits the club and submits the reimbursement as a meal expense. Unless auditors recognize the names of the clubs, there is no obvious red flag of the event.

In a recent case, the *Wall Street Journal* reported on an executive who entertained customers at a gentlemen's club. The event caused adverse publicity for the company. Adverse publicity can be a greater risk than the loss of assets.

Rental Car Receipt Scheme   In this scheme, the traveler rents an automobile for sightseeing rather than for business. The red flag is that the miles driven are not consistent with the intended business purpose. In addition, the gas reimbursement is not consistent with the miles driven.

Taxicab Receipt Scheme   This scheme occurs because cab drivers may provide several blank receipts to the traveler. Therefore; auditors should be alert to the reasonableness of the amount, and whether a second traveler also submitted a receipt for the same expenditure.

10

Payroll Fraud Schemes

Payroll fraud by its essence is an uncomplicated scheme. However, finding the fraudulent transaction and, subsequently, proving the payroll fraud can be difficult because of the dollar magnitude and volume of transactions involved with the payroll cycle. The two typical inherent fraud schemes are associated with ghost employees and time reporting fraud. In addition, payroll calculation schemes concerning the payroll office occur, but on a less frequent basis.

GHOST EMPLOYEES

"Ghost employees" are individuals listed in the payroll register, who are not providing services, but who are receiving a payroll check. The generic fraud scheme requires the ability to place an individual or retain a terminated employee on the payroll system, falsify the time and attendance reporting, and divert the payroll payment. The conversion cycle occurs through the diversion of the payroll payment or collusion with an employee receiving the paycheck.

Variations of Ghost Employees

There are eight typical variations of the inherent ghost employee fraud scheme.

1. **Fictitious employee.** The employee is placed on the payroll system, allowing the supervisor to falsify time reporting, and then, a payroll check is diverted or the payment is directly deposited into a false

bank account. Data mining for fictitious employees would focus on these data elements:

- ○ High withholding exemptions or no withholding for income taxes

- ○ No voluntary deductions for health insurance, retirement, or other normal deductions for the employee population

- ○ No vacation, sick, or personal time charges

- ○ No salary adjustments, merit adjustments, or promotions

- ○ Duplicate bank account numbers

- ○ Matching to other logical databases, e.g., security access, computer security access file or company telephone records

Audit Strategy:
- ○ For each person, meet the individual and inspect government-issued identification.

- ○ Search for evidence of work performance. This may be as simple as inspecting employee's work area.

2. **Terminated ghost employee scheme.** The employee exists at the time of hiring, but terminates employment without notifying human resources. The supervisor falsifies the time report, indicating that the employee is working, and diverts the employee's payment. The terminated employee may remain on the payroll system indefinitely, especially if they do not question year-end payroll statements. However, the supervisor may remove the employee after diverting a few payroll checks, if the employee receives and questions the year-end payroll statement. Data mining for terminated ghost employees would focus on these data elements:

- ○ Change to direct deposit bank account information

- ○ Endorsements on payroll checks

- ○ Terminated status

Audit Strategy:
- ○ Compare endorsement on the check for the last payroll period to the first payroll period.

- ○ Compare handwriting on the final time report to the first time report

3. **Pre-employment ghost employee scheme.** This scheme occurs when a supervisor places the employee on the payroll system one

pay period before the actual commencement of services. The scheme occurs with employees who are not likely to question a payroll reporting statement. The data mining would focus on new employees and date of first payment.

Audit Strategy:
- ○ Compare first payment week to other relevant databases to establish a work performance date.
- ○ Interview employees to determine their recollection of their first day or week of work.

4. **No-show ghost employee scheme.** This scheme occurs when an employee, who is a real person, provides no actual services. The no-show ghost employee is typically in collusion with a supervisor. Since the individual is a real person, data-mining steps are limited. Treating the no-show ghost employee in the same manner as a fictitious employee may provide positive results.

Audit Strategy:
- ○ Search for evidence of work performance.
- ○ Interview coworkers.
- ○ Examine access security databases for evidence of work performance.

5. **Temporary employees bypass critical hiring controls.** These employees exist, but because of the temporary nature of their employment, hiring controls may be bypassed. Control over temporary employees is usually vested with the local manager making such bypassing uncomplicated. Data mining for temporary employees focuses on those coded in the system as temporary or as employees with short durations of employment.

Audit Strategy:
- ○ Confirm the existence of the employee through a telephone interview.
- ○ Search for evidence of work performance.
- ○ Interview coworkers.

6. **Temporary employees working through agencies.** These individuals bypass the hiring process because they are not employees of the organization. The temporary agency is in collusion with human resources or the requesting manager. The requesting manager approves the invoice indicating the individuals were present and worked the days

noted on the vendor invoice. In essence, the agency bills the company for individuals who did not provide services. The agency provides a kickback to the company employee who approves the charge. Data mining for temporary employees focuses on identifying departments incurring temporary agency expense via general ledger review.

Audit Strategy:
- ○ Examine temporary agency payroll records to ensure that the individual was compensated and that time records support the work location.

- ○ Search for evidence of work performance.

7. **Family member ghost employees.** In closely held corporations, owners may place family members on the payroll to minimize taxes or divert funds for other personal reasons. Data mining for family member ghost employees focuses on employees with common names, addresses, telephone numbers, or bank account information.

Audit Strategy:
- ○ Search for evidence of work performance.

8. **Unclaimed payroll check scheme.** This scheme involves the theft of an unclaimed payroll check. It may occur with a recently terminated employee or by diverting a stale payroll check once it becomes obvious that no employee will collect it. Data mining considerations involve reviewing bank reconciliations for outstanding payroll checks that subsequently clear.

Audit Strategy:
- ○ Examine checks for false endorsements.

- ○ Compare bank clearing stamps on early checks to last check to see if the bank used to negotiate check has changed.

Finding Ghost Employees

Due to the large number of employees, the geographic spread of companies, and multiple work shifts, auditors need to develop a data-mining strategy to search for ghost employees. Ghost employees tend to occur in departments where they would not be evident, and the local manager has a high degree of control over the hiring process. These characteristics are useful in the search for the ghost employee.

Department Characteristics that Facilitate Ghost Employees In cases where the nature of a department facilitates the concealing of ghost employees, the following departmental characteristics should be considered:

- Decentralized, remote departments that have low visibility employees
- Departments that experience regular turnover
- Department or locations that are managed by an individual with a high degree of authority
- Departments where employees are more likely to collude to conceal a ghost employee
- Entry-level positions
- Departments with employees who work remotely
- Departments where payroll budget and actual payroll expenditures would normally differ
- Large departments where a ghost employee would not be evident

As a reminder, there are no absolutes. However, these questions are useful in identifying departments where ghost employees are more likely to be used in a payroll fraud scheme:

- Who has the ability to place an individual on the payroll?
- Are any employees hired directly by a hiring supervisor?
- Does a hiring supervisor verify the existence or identity of new employees?
- Do any employees bypass an interview with human resources?
- Does any department submit employee forms or start requests directly to human resources?
- Do any employees terminate without an exit conference with human resources?
- Can one individual place an employee on the payroll system without a second review or reconciliation?
- Does the manager approving the payroll change have the necessary knowledge to identify a fictitious employee?
- Do employees know to notify human resources regarding termination benefits and rights?

The Red Flags of Ghost Employees

- Use of a common name, e.g., Smith

- No physical address

- No personal or vacation leave

- No deductions for voluntary deductions (i.e., health insurance, pension, etc.)

- High withholding allowance to minimize income tax withholding

- Missing employee information

- Invalid social security numbers

- IRS notice regarding invalid social security numbers

- No evidence of work performance

- Changes to direct deposit bank account numbers

- Payroll checks that are cashed in company accounts

- Duplicate bank accounts for direct deposits

Ghost Employee Characteristics   The nature of an employee's work status facilitates the concealing of ghost employees. Consider the following employee types:

- Employees who work remotely, so, no one in the company sees them

- Foreign nationals, where the supervisor simply states that, to the best of their knowledge, the employee has returned to the country of origin

- Employees who would bypass normal hiring or termination controls, because the supervisor maintains a high degree of control over employees

- Transient employees, because they typically work for a limited period of time and then move to a different geographic area

Another way to identify ghost employees is to identify opportunities that allow for the diversion of the payroll payment. The characteristics associated with payroll check diversion are:

- Payroll checks are delivered to the supervisor.

- Direct deposits are established for employees that bypass normal hiring practices.

- Direct deposit changes are allowed without independent verification.

- Poor controls exist regarding unclaimed payroll checks.

Audit Procedures for Ghost Employees The six audit procedures for ghost employees are:

1. Examine employees' government identification documents.

2. Compare their employees' government identification to known true government identification for signs of alteration or creation.

3. Obtain employee files to identify documents and handwriting.

4. Interview employees regarding their department or job duties.

5. Examine documents for evidence of job performance.

6. Examine other logical databases for performance:

   a. Computer sign-on/off

   b. Telephone records

   c. Security systems

OVERTIME REPORTING FRAUD

Overtime reporting fraud occurs, when employees falsify the hours worked, or due to a breakdown in the time card approval process. The conversion occurs through the employee's payroll check or a kickback to a second person operating in collusion with the employee. Overstated hours fraud can also occur when part-time employees are paid for more hours worked, but not exceeding the typical full-time standard of 40 hours.

The variations for the misstated hours occur in these ways:

- Employees misstate hours piecemeal, and supervisors approve the hours unknowingly.

- Employees operate in collusion to misstate each other's hours, and supervisors approve the hours unknowingly.

- An employee misstates hours in collusion with the supervisor. The supervisor falsely approves the hours and receives a kickback from the employee. The supervisor could also be motivated to provide disguised compensation to the employee for any number of reasons.

- Employees forge the approval of their supervisor on their time cards.

- Employees alter their time cards after the supervisor properly approves the cards. The control breakdown occurs by the employees obtaining access to properly approved time cards.
- A payroll employee overstates their hours on a properly approved time card.

The opportunity for time card fraud is enhanced when:

- Supervisors do not have firsthand knowledge of an employee's workday.
- Supervisors believe that overtime is a method to provide additional compensation to key employees.
- Properly approved time cards are returned to an employee.
- Employees complete manual time cards.
- There are staggered stop and start time employees on a work shift.
- Employees work in the field without reporting to a central office.

Typically, the examination of time cards does not detect overtime fraud, because the hours are reported and the cards are approved. However, auditors should be on the lookout for alterations and false approvals. To detect time card fraud, auditors need to identify a database that records work times. Then, the auditors can compare the hours on the time card to the hours on the independent database. Auditors should access security logs, computer sign-on and off logs, and telephone records; and parking lot registers are all useful for matching purposes. If no database is available, detecting time card fraud through standard audit procedures can be difficult.

Other verification procedures are:

- Interview employees in the department who did not receive overtime regarding department work schedules.
- Set up surveillance of suspected departments.
- Perform surprise inspection of work areas and examine the reported hours on that day.

FRAUD OPPORTUNITIES IN THE PAYROLL OFFICE

The payroll office is the ultimate gatekeeper regarding payroll internal controls and, correspondingly, has the greatest fraud opportunity. A properly completed and approved time card can be altered by the payroll clerk and processed for higher hours. The clerk can simply discard the time card stating 40 hours and pay a friend for 60 hours instead. In addition, salary change forms could be processed at a higher rate than approved.

Payroll Calculation Fraud Schemes

Employees' compensation can be falsely calculated by using false grades, pay scales, or annual salary amounts. Once the false information is entered into the computer, the calculation becomes automatic. Within the payroll system, several database fields or subsystems allow for increasing weekly pay or other forms of compensation. A description of those fraud opportunities follows.

- **Salary adjustment field.** In the payroll database, a field exists for providing an employee a manually calculated lump-sum adjustment. Retroactive merit adjustments are common examples. In addition, the field can be used to provide fraudulent adjustments to an employee. For example, a payroll clerk can provide themselves, or an employee, a false adjustment. Data-mining procedures should be used to search for employees receiving more than one adjustment.

    In one case, a manager provided an employee with 52 weekly salary adjustments for local travel. Upon further investigation, it was found that the manager was bypassing the compensation system controls by increasing the employee's gross compensation beyond the salary level for the particular job grade.

- **"Other" salary adjustment field.** Databases often include a category or field called "other." Other database fields exist to provide employees' payments for various reimbursements:
    ○ Employee incentive bonus
    ○ Other reimbursements
    ○ Local travel reimbursements
    ○ Allowance programs

    Auditors should verify salary adjustments against the original source documents, independently verify the reason for the adjustment, and recalculate the salary amount.

- **Manual payroll checks.** There are a variety of reasons to provide an employee with a manual payroll check. A termination paycheck is one example.

    In one case, a controller issued himself 52 automated checks and 8 manual payroll checks. The manual checks were recorded to a non-payroll general ledger account through a journal entry.

- **Other compensation fields.** Various data fields influence retirement, health benefits, and personal leave calculations. The altering of any of these fields would provide an employee with other compensation benefits.

Fringe Benefit–Related Schemes

Health insurance has become a valuable benefit for employees. Yet, very few companies reconcile the total number of employees receiving health insurance to the active payroll or to COBRA benefits to terminated employees.[1] Since family health coverage exceeds $10,000 per year, the benefit is a prime target for fraud. The scheme is simple and operates in the following ways:

- The health insurance administrator provides a nonemployee with health insurance coverage.

- An employee claims a nondependent on the coverage or an employee falsely claims that a live-in companion is a spouse.

- The COBRA benefit period is falsely extended for terminated employees.

Other fringe benefit–related schemes are associated with false reimbursement for benefits or allowances. The fraud occurs by the employee submitting false documents or the payroll employee falsely providing the employee with the payment.

Misuse-of-Employees Schemes

In misuse-of-employees schemes, the employee performs no job-related duties. Examples of the misuse of employees include using employees in political campaigns, for personal errands, or for other activities. Since there is no record of the misuse, typically, the frauds are revealed by whistleblowers.

Sales Commissions and Bonus Schemes

Sales representatives, who are paid on sales performance, have the opportunity to manipulate sales activities to increase their compensation in a number of ways. They can:

---

[1]COBRA, the Consolidated Omnibus Budget Reconciliation Act, is a government mandate that allows terminated employees the right to continue to purchase their health benefits for a certain period after termination.

- **Book fictitious year-end sales.** Reasons for booking these sales might be to achieve sales quotas and obtain bonuses or to attend key sales meetings. Auditors should scrutinize returns and adjustments in the next period.

- **Change quotas to allow a sales representative to receive a bonus.** Typically, this scheme is performed by the sales manager. The manager receives a kickback from the sales representative out of the false bonus. Auditors should compare end-of-the-year quotas to beginning-of-the-year quotas to identify potential fraudulent changes. Auditors should ensure that any changes were approved and that the reason for the change was valid and authorized by a manager above the approving manager level.

- **Providing customers with false benefits.** In this scheme, the sales representative receives a kickback from the customers.

- **Providing customers with false credits on unsold goods.** The sales representative receives a kickback from the customer or the customer purchases additional items allowing the sales representative to earn commissions.

- **Selling sales promotional items.** The sales representative simply keeps the money from the sale.

Innovative Fraud   Sales representatives' compensation is based on sales performance and maximizing the interpretation of the commission program. Sales representatives have come up with clever techniques to increase their compensation.

In one such scheme, a sales representative sold an item to a customer and, then provided the customer with the money to pay for the item. The sale allowed the representative to earn a bonus.

In another scheme, a publishing company was experiencing a drop in subscription sales. The company implemented a new commission program to compensate salespeople for getting customers to renew their subscription. However, one salesperson convinced customers to let their subscription lapse for one period. The salesperson would rewrite a sales order for the subscription. The customer would receive a one-year discount on the subscription, and the sales representative would receive a commission.

Diversion of Payroll Tax Deposits

In small businesses, a common fraud is the theft of payroll tax deposits. The payroll clerk diverts the check for their own benefit. The concealment occurs because of the overreliance by the owner on the payroll clerk and, so, the payroll clerk handles all government notices. The accountant may also miss the scheme because net payroll and the alleged tax payments reconcile to the gross payroll. The fraud is detected when the government becomes aggressive in the collection of the delinquent tax payments. Auditors should ensure that the canceled check for the taxes was deposited in the proper tax account.

11

Revenue Fraud

How fraud in the revenue and cash receipt cycle occurs in an organization depends largely on the nature of the business and how the revenue cycle operates. In a fraud risk assessment, auditors will start with the inherent fraud schemes described in this chapter and then think about how and where each scheme could occur in the organization. Unlike the expenditure cycle, the mechanics of the fraud scheme will vary by organization.

For simplicity, the term "cash receipts" is used to refer to incoming funds that are currency, customer checks, wire transfers, and credit cards. When the discussion focuses on a specific form of tender, the text will specify the source of funds.

EMBEZZLEMENT OF CASH RECEIPTS

There are specific fraud schemes related to cash receipts exclusively. Typically, the schemes occur with cash receipts before recording sales, after initial recording sales, and from nonrevenue sources. Typically, schemes involving the embezzlement of cash receipts are known as skimming schemes.

Before Recording Sales

The embezzlement of cash receipts fraud scheme is referred to as a skimming scheme. The fraud occurs by the theft of incoming customer payments or of nonrevenue cash receipts before the funds are deposited and recorded in the accounting records. The scheme requires an individual to receive the funds and avoid the accountability controls. The concealment strategy to hide the theft varies by the nature of the incoming funds and the perpetrators' responsibilities and authority. The typical concealment strategies are:

- **No one will miss the funds.** In a retail environment, there is no record of the sales transaction or the theft if the cashier diverts the customer payment without recording the sale in the cash register.

- **Controlling the communication with the customer.** A life insurance agent or investment advisor receives funds directly from a customer. If the representative diverts the funds and provides the customer with false statements, the fraud will continue until a mistake occurs or a customer attempts to collect the funds and the perpetrator cannot provide the funds.

- **Responsibility for explaining the unfavorable variations or discrepancies.** The theft of funds should create an unfavorable variance, such as a decrease in the gross profit. If the local manager is responsible for explaining the variance, he or she could divert the funds and provide false explanations.

Understanding the conversion cycle is important in recognition of the ease in which the skimming scheme occurs. Revenue skimming typically happens with the theft of currency, because no skills are required to convert the funds to personal benefit. However, customer checks can be negotiated through the following:

- An accomplice at a bank who is willing to negotiate the check

- Establishing a false bank account with a look-alike name

- Negotiating the check at a dishonest money service bureau

From an audit theory perspective, this scheme is generally not detectable by traditional sampling and audit procedures, because the transaction is not recorded. Therefore, auditors must understand that not all fraud schemes are detectable by traditional tests of controls. Fraud analytics may be useful in detecting the probability of skimming, but investigative procedures will be required to track the theft.

Fraud analytics should focus on the concealment strategy being employed by the perpetrator. With the concealment strategy in mind, the auditors' analysis should focus on the composition of daily deposits, specifically, currency, customer checks, credit cards, or wire transfers. The auditor is searching for a change in the composition of the daily deposits correlated to an event or person. The nature of the change is the red flag, and the response will be dictated by the nature of the change. Skimming also results in a reduction of gross profit. In many skimming schemes, the change in gross profit is negligible at the organizational level. The best chance of identifying the change in gross profit is to perform a disaggregated analysis by product line.

Example

In one fraud case, a company was comprised of 15 operating locations. The gross profit on an organizational level did not indicate a negative change. However, at one of the smaller operating units, the gross profit decreased by 15 percent. Further analysis indicated that the major product line had a minor change in gross profit, which could be explained by many different lines. However, in the minor product lines, the negative change in the gross profit was 100 percent. Where was the skimming scheme taking place? From a concealment point, substantiating or refuting the representations for the changes caused by theft point is the best approach for auditors in answering this question. When the auditor refutes the employee's explanations, the perpetrator of the crime might confess.

After Initial Recording of Sales

Once the sales transaction is recorded, the perpetrator must conceal the theft of cash receipts through another recorded transaction. The altering transaction can be a credit, void, return, dormant credit, or journal entry. The key is to link the altering transaction to the theft of the cash receipt. The red flag of the theft is the altering transaction. The pattern or frequency of the altering transaction is the anomaly in the cycle. The pattern may be associated with a person or an account. The frequency is the number of occurrences that exceeds the norm for the sales activity.

The theft of cash receipts can be concealed with collusion. For example, assume the individual receiving the funds diverts the payments. In collusion with a customer service representative, dormant or aged customer credits are identified and applied to the customer's account in which the funds were embezzled.

Cash Receipts from Nonrevenue Sources

It is very common for cash receipts to be received directly by internal employees. For example, risk management receives cash receipts for insurance claims, human resources receives cash receipts for COBRA health insurance payments, credit and collections receive cash receipts for bad debt customers, and purchasing receives volume discount payments. Each one of these functions is well suited to divert the cash receipt and conceal the theft. In the search for fraud opportunity, the handling of nonrevenue cash receipts is a prime area for review.

The audit approach follows:

1. Identify the departments that are receiving cash receipts directly.

2. Identify the source of the funds and request the source to provide a listing of payments.

3. Trace the payments into the accounting records. If there are missing payments, you most likely have uncovered a fraud.

OTHER EMBEZZLEMENT SCHEMES

Currency Substitution Schemes

The perpetrator of currency substitution schemes diverts the incoming currency and conceals the theft by holding back customer checks and depositing the checks at a later time. The concealment strategy is intended to provide the illusion of daily deposits being made at a constant level. In addition, false coupons, vouchers, or providing other false documentation as evidence of the funds hide the theft of currency. The red flag is when currency as a percentage of the daily deposits decreases throughout the theft period until the daily deposits are comprised solely of checks or credit cards.

Embezzlement Concealed with a Lapping

"Lapping" is a concealment strategy to conceal the theft of a customer's payment. The theft starts with the embezzlement of a payment associated with a customer's accounts receivable balance. In the traditional scheme, the perpetrator has access to both incoming funds and the accounts receivable records. The theft of one customer check is concealed by applying another customer check to first customer's account. Once started, the fraud scheme typically continues until the perpetrator is caught. It is easy to see how this becomes a variation of the well-known pyramid scheme. This scheme is most likely to occur in small businesses in which there is not an adequate separation of duties.

The scheme occurs in larger companies if someone in cash management operates in collusion within someone else with the capability to issue credits or cause transfers of credits.

Data Mining for Lapping   Identifying the scheme is a relatively easy, with data mining, using the following steps:

1. Compare the customer remittance number from one month to the next month.

2. Compute a net change between the numbers.

3. Then look for an illogical change in customer remittance numbers. For example, assume that the January customer remittance number was 10500 and the February customer remittance number was 4567. Since customer check numbers typically increase, the negative net change would be a red flag. Remember, red flags do not equal fraud; they just mean that the transaction fits the fraud profile. Other red flags of lapping are:

   ○ Transfers of credits between unrelated customers

   ○ Delayed posting of customer payments

   ○ Missing customer remittance advices

   ○ Undocumented credit adjustments

   ○ Customer inquiries regarding unapplied payments

Lapping in Nonaccounts Receivable   The fraud concept is important and can be applied to other operating areas. The fundamental theory is that the theft of funds is being concealed with funds from another source. The next examples illustrate how the lapping theory can be used to conceal a fraud scheme.

In a loan fraud scheme involving notes of short duration, the loan officer embezzled the funds by establishing a fictitious customer. At the end of the note period, the loan officer rolled the note for a new 60-day period. The new loan was for the original loan amount plus interest. In this variation, the loan officer was lapping with the bank's funds, not with a customer's payment.

Theft of Product for Resale Scheme

The theft of product for resale fraud scheme involves the theft of company inventory for resale. The fraud scheme is not a true revenue scheme but rather an inventory scheme. Sales representatives could also sell samples of company products and retain the proceeds. The sale of scrap by employees is a common scheme. Typically, these cases become known through tips or hot lines.

Front Customer Schemes

As in the vendor scheme, a company employee establishes a front company. The front company, functioning as an arm's-length customer, purchases items at favorable terms or prices and then resells the items in direct competition with the subject company. Company employees using their positions of influence sell the item to the front company at a lower price than normal. The favorable pricing is concealed with a false representation. The goods are shipped to the front company or the front company directs the shipment to its customer. Once the front company receives payment from the customer, it pays its receivable balance, completing the revenue cycle.

The first fraud is a conflict of interest by company employees competing directly with their employer. The second aspect is the selling of the item at favorable pricing for personal gain. Adding insult to injury can occur when the company employees receive a commission or bonus on the original sale. Potential red flags are:

- Rapid change in credit limits
- Multiple ship-to addresses with different customer names
- Continual slow paying
- Favorable pricing, discounts, or sales adjustments

Favored Terms Schemes

In these schemes, the customer receives terms that are more favorable than they ordinarily would receive. The customer pays a bribe or kickback to the company employee for the favorable treatment. Whatever the benefit, the salesperson provides favorable terms, pricing, and/or payment terms to the customer to the detriment of the company.

The scheme also operates by selling to customers who are not creditworthy or continuing to ship goods to customers who are delinquent in their payments. The company representative authorizes the decision based on false representations and receives a bribe for the favorable treatment. In the banking world, many loan frauds occur due to the issuance of loan based on false pretenses.

Sales Returns and Adjustments Schemes

In these schemes, false adjustments are created and issued to a customer's account. The credits can be transferred to an account controlled by the perpetrator, or the perpetrator receives a kickback from the customer. The red flag is the frequency and dollar amount of returns and adjustments by the customer. In addition, the adjustments may be used to hide a poor credit decision by a company employee.

In a retail environment, a store clerk was creating false returns and providing a credit to her personal credit card. Another scheme had to do with products that had an expiration date. The returned products resulted in a chargeback that was verified by the sales representative. However, the sales representative was falsely certifying the chargeback and receiving a kickback from the customer.

Fictitious Customer Refunds

The fictitious customer refunds fraud scheme involves the theft of customer refunds. How the scheme occurs depends on the organization. Two possibilities follow:

- A customer service representative scans the accounts receivable and identifies dormant credits or dormant credit balances. Knowing that the customer has most likely forgotten about the credit, the representative creates a fictitious request from the customer to change their address. Once the address change has occurred, a second fictitious request is submitted requesting a refund of the credits. Accounting researches the customer's request, notes a credit balance, and issues a check to the customer. Unfortunately, the address is controlled by the customer service representative.

- False adjustments are provided to a customer's account. Once the credits are applied, the customer requests a refund and provides a kickback to the company employee who created the false credit.

Customer Blow-Out Scheme

In this scheme, customers purchase items with no intent of paying for them. The scheme starts with customers purchasing items and establishing a good payment history. At some point, they increase their purchases by a substantial amount. Then they close up their operation and flee the area without paying. The scheme could occur in collusion with a company employee or by the customer alone. This scheme is a typical fraud scheme in a bankruptcy cases.

Delinquent Customer Bail-Out Scheme

In the delinquent customer bail-Out scheme, a manager in credit and collection identifies a customer in severe arrears. The customer is about to be closed out for future purchases from the company. Without access to the company's product, the customer would go out of business. An individual in collusion with the credit and collection manager approaches the customer, offering to assist the customer in developing a plan to repay the delinquent purchases while continuing to buy from the company. The delinquent customer pays the individual a fee for these services. The individual then splits the fee with the credit and collection manager.

Theft of Payments from a Bad-Debt Customer

In this scheme, a manager diverts the payment from a bad-debt customer. Then, the bad debt customer is written off without their knowledge. The manager then sets up the delinquent customer under a new name and address. The scheme could also occur with collusion between the customer and the credit and collection manager.

12

Asset Fraud Schemes

Auditors typically view property and equipment as a low-risk area. However, the opportunity for a significant fraud in a one-time transaction is actually high. The purchase of a building at an inflated price from a related party can cause significant losses. Long-term leases with an undisclosed senior manager can cause adverse publicity to the corporation. The misuse of corporate assets by a senior executive may be indicative of a disguised compensation scheme, or a case of bribery where the funds may be used to bribe government officials. The nature of these schemes requires greater scrutiny by auditors.

THEFT OF ASSETS

One popular fraud scheme is the theft of assets associated with employees. Vendors and outside parties also may be involved in these schemes, but that is beyond the scope of this text. Audits of asset theft cases involve two parts:

1. Establish the internal employee responsible for the theft of the asset.
2. Determine the extent of the loss attributable to the theft.

The strategies for auditing theft are to catch the person in the act of the theft, obtain a confession from the party, obtain statements from witnesses, or obtain a statement from the person who purchased the asset from the perpetrator. The nature of the scheme does not lend itself to normal auditing techniques. Typically, investigative techniques are required.

Once an audit begins, the perpetrator is put on notice that the scheme has been detected. At that point, the perpetrator typically stops stealing.

Unlike an embezzlement case were the fraudulent act is documented in the business records, once the person stops stealing, catching him or her in the act becomes difficult.

The red flags of theft vary by the nature of the scheme, but some typical signs include:

- Inventory variances resulting from physical counts
- Stock outages when the inventory records indicate sufficient quantities
- Drops in margins

The concealment of the theft will vary by the nature of the asset taken in a theft scheme. Concealment can include write-off of the asset as scrap, obsolescence, missing, donated, or destroyed. These normal day-to-day business activities can be used to conceal the theft of assets:

- Write-off of the asset through shrinkage
- Assets that are used in the normal course of business
- Labeling the movement of the asset as customer adjustment, no charge, promotional, transfer, or internal consumption
- Movement of assets between two control points with no documentation supporting the transfer
- Acceptance of goods without documentation or creating false documentation to support the receipt of the goods
- Creating false work orders
- Creating false receiving reports as to quantity, quality, or specifications (Assets that are consumed in the course of normal business are susceptible to this concealment strategy.)
- Creating fictitious credits to hide the shortage
- Nonbilling of the asset sale
- False inventory counts or alteration of records after the physical count

Theft Audit Cycle

Understanding the theft cycle is the key to investigating the occurrence of the fraud scheme. A discussion of the stages of the theft cycle follows.

- **Theft.** "Theft" is defined as the physical movement of the asset from the company to the employee's control. Employees may remove the asset:
  - In the normal course of their duties

- During normal work hours
- In an off-hour scheme

- **Theft point.** Assets may be diverted before or after the company takes possession. If the asset is diverted before possession, it usually is indicative of weaknesses in the receiving function. Diversion after possession is indicative of weaknesses in physical security controls.

- **Parties to theft.** The theft may occur through employees, an accomplice, or a fictitious vendor or customer.

- **Concealment.** This stage refers to how employees conceal the theft or misuse of the asset. The schemes range from nothing to creating internal documents to reflect a sale, transfer, or obsolescence of an asset.

- **Time.** The amount of time between the theft and identification of the loss is a subset of the concealment phase.

- **Normal course of business.** Supplies and inventory by their nature are consumed in the normal course of business. The consumption of the product becomes part of the concealment because the asset cannot be examined.

- **Conversion.** In this phase, employees convert the asset to economic gain. In misuse cases, the conversion is the use of the asset. In theft, the conversion is the personal use or resale of the asset.

- **Likelihood.** Auditors are not searching for the employee who uses a company pencil for personal use. Auditors need to assess whether an employee or group of employees could divert significant assets.

- **Opportunity.** The type, nature, and extent of the asset conversion will impact this phase. In the simplest form, the employee walks out of the company with the asset.

- **Misuse.** "Misuse" refers to business assets that are used for personal use or to bribe customers or government officials. In government contracts, the asset is purchased for a specific purpose but is used for nongovernmental contract purposes. These areas are typical for misuse fraud cases:
  - Real estate, such as apartments and storage facilities
  - Transportation assets, such as vehicles, air transportation, or boat transportation
  - Office equipment
  - Equipment and tools
  - Assets used in other businesses

OTHER ASSET FRAUD SCHEMES

Some typical fraud schemes associated with assets are highlighted below.

No Business Use of the Asset Scheme

In this scheme, the asset acquired has no legitimate business purpose. The asset may be a disguised compensation scheme for a senior executive or an asset used to bribe customers or politicians. Auditors should search for assets or leases that would have a personal inurement value. The audit procedure is to inquire as to use, inspect the assets, or the verify logs documenting the use.

Excessive Expenditure Scheme

In this fraud scheme, the asset is acquired for a valid business purposes, but its cost exceeds the utility requirement of the organization. The New York City apartment in the Tyco case illustrates this fraud scheme. In terms of executive management, the Tyco scheme is a form of disguised compensation. The audit procedure is to determine by whom and how the asset is being used, understand the comparable costs, and ensure there is a reporting mechanism for the use of the asset.

Asset Purchase Scheme

In the asset purchase scheme, the asset is acquired from a related party without disclosure at an inflated price. Real estate flips are often associated with this scheme. The property changes hands several times to artificially increase the perception of the market value. This scheme is associated with kickback schemes. The audit procedure is to focus on the sales history of the asset and to what parties.

Asset Retirement Scheme

In an asset retirement scheme, the asset is intentionally sold below fair market value. The purchaser then either retains it for personal use or resells it at fair market value. Company automobiles are often associated with this fraud scheme. In one instance, a company-leased vehicle had zero miles usage for the two-year lease. The manager responsible for the lease purchased the car from the vendor at the end of the lease period. In essence he purchased a new car at a price of a two-year-old car.

13

Fraud Control Theory

Using a variation of a saying from the 1960s, fraud happens. Like all costs of doing business, fraud must be managed. Management must recognize that people commit fraudulent acts because of the pressures and rationalization aspects of the fraud theory. The control opportunity provides people with the ability to commit the acts. Due to the concealment or trickery aspect of the fraud theory, fraud occurs in both poorly managed and well-managed departments. Organizations need to talk about fraud, not merely hope that it will not happen. The antifraud program in all organizations needs to remain alert and diligent to fraud.

A key element of the control environment theory is commitment to competence. It is interesting that management is responsible for fraud prevention but most likely has never received training in fraud or internal controls. To achieve the commitment to competence, management needs to be trained in fundamental fraud theory and fraud prevention strategies.

Control inhibitors provide the illusion that a control is operating. However, the perpetrator has circumvented the control, thereby committing the fraud scheme without detection. The control inhibitors are real and do occur. These examples illustrate the concept of internal control inhibitors:

- Management override is most likely the number-one reason for major frauds. Management override consists of both the act of override and the lack of scrutiny in the performance of their control responsibilities.

- Collusion among employees, customers, and vendors does occur. In fact, many fraud schemes require collusion. The act of bribery is the perfect example. People do not bribe themselves.

- Nonperformance or lack of understanding of internal controls negates the value of the internal controls.
- Falsified documents conceal fraud.

ANTIFRAUD PROGRAMS

The cornerstones of managing the cost of fraud are recognizing the need for an antifraud program and ensuring that the identified fraud risks have the appropriate balance of internal controls to manage the fraud cost.

The best practice for fraud prevention is for an organization to have an effective and visible antifraud program. The program should be linked to the control model used by the organization. Using the COSO (Committee of Sponsoring Organizations) model, the components of the antifraud program are:

- Performing fraud risk assessments
- Creating a control environment adverse to fraud
- Designing and implementing antifraud control activities
- Sharing information and communication
- Monitoring activities
- Responding to fraudulent activities

Statement of Auditing Standards No. 99 provides a 14-point antifraud program as an attachment to the standard. The framework centers on these three principles:

1. Creating a culture of honesty and high ethics
2. Evaluating antifraud processes and controls
3. Developing an appropriate oversight process

Performing Fraud Risk Assessments

The first step in creating an antifraud program is to ensure that management understands where the organization is vulnerable to the risk of fraud. Management is clearly responsible for the overall effectiveness of the fraud risk assessment. The risk assessment should document the inherent fraud risks, describe the exposures, and link the internal control strategy to the fraud risk.

Creating a Control Environment

The control environment should set the proper tone at the top. The control environment, or soft controls, influences the effectiveness of the control procedures. Employees quickly understand which internal controls are important to management and which internal controls receive less attention from management. Therefore, the control environment should:

- Create and maintain a culture of honesty and ethical business standards

- Provide discipline for violations of the code of conduct (In other words, there should be consequences for employees' actions.)

- Communicate the appropriate tone regarding tolerance toward fraudulent activities

- Establish control procedures and policies to prevent, detect, and deter fraud

- Establish an assertive policy regarding auditing and investigating fraud

Remember, it must be more than just a policy statement. Management must walk the talk. Actions speak more than the words of a policy statement.

Designing and Implementing Antifraud Control Activities

Internal control procedures should be linked to the fraud risks identified in the fraud risk assessment. The goal is to mitigate the fraud risks consistent with management's goal and desire to minimize fraud to an acceptable level. The controls are referred to as preventive and detective controls. The system of controls should also consider managing the control inhibitors, which often override the fundamental control activities.

Sharing Information and Communicating

The company's code of conduct and the organization fraud response policy are the keys to communicating the organization's no-tolerance attitude toward fraudulent and unethical business practices. It is more than just having a policy. The company's position must be communicated on a regular basis using company newsletters and handbooks, online messages, and training and management presentations. Fraud awareness is an important aspect of the antifraud program.

Monitoring Activities

A key component of an antifraud program is to increase the perception of detection of fraudulent activities. Fraud monitoring systems and reports are effective tools to accomplish the goal. The systems should be built around the inherent fraud schemes identified in the fraud risk assessment. In chapters one through five, we discussed the use of red flags to identify various fraud schemes. Using the red flag approach, management can develop reports to identify transactions consistent with the fraud data profile.

A second aspect of the program consists of annual independent evaluations of the antifraud program. A consistent and credible antifraud program becomes a deterrent to individuals who are contemplating committing fraudulent activities.

Responding to Fraudulent Activities

When allegations of fraud occur, management needs the ability to respond to the allegations. The use of a fraud response policy is the cornerstone of the program. Chapter 15 covers the components of the policy. The organization also needs access to auditors with specialized skills to identify fraudulent activities within the normal course of audits and to properly investigate fraud allegations. The use of internal auditors, an external accounting firm, or specialized consultants are critical to the ongoing effectiveness of the program.

FRAUD CONTROL AND COSO

According to the COSO model, control procedures are a key element to mitigate risks. A control matrix is an effective tool to document the fraud control procedures. The process starts with the identified fraud risk and links the fraud prevention, fraud detection, and deterrence controls to the fraud risk.

Fraud Prevention and Control Procedures

Preventive controls are designed to minimize the likelihood of a fraud risk from occurring in a business system. The Control Activities section of the COSO model provides for the completeness and authorization of internal control procedures. Although found in older internal control theory, the concept of disciplinary controls is vital to fraud prevention. Disciplinary controls are internal controls that are intended to ensure that the control procedures are operating as intended by management. The appropriate separation of duties is the perfect example for disciplinary controls. No one individual has responsibility for all aspects of the business process. At the organizational level, the internal audit department functions as a regulator of the internal controls process.

Fraud Detection Procedures

Detective controls are designed to alert management that a fraud risk is occurring on a timely basis. The Monitoring, Supervision and Information and Communication section of the COSO model provides for the fraud detection procedures. Properly designed fraud monitoring controls can act as both a deterrent and detection control. Auditors use the red flag theory for fraud identification. Logically management should use the same fraud theory to increase its ability to monitor business transactions.

In many systems, a transaction reporting listing all changes is produced and reviewed. A manager initials the monitoring report indicating review and approval. The problem with the report is the volume of changes and the cursory review performed by many managers.

Monitoring controls, built around the fraud scheme, function as deterrents by making fraud schemes visible. Monitoring reports should not be kept secret. Employees in the processing function should be advised of the reports. The reports should be reviewed by someone other than the processing employee's immediate supervisor. This procedure diminishes the exposure to logical collusion.

In bid avoidance schemes, a false representation regarding sole-source decision is a fraud strategy to influence the awarding of a contract. Requiring all sole-source contracts exceeding a predetermined dollar amount to be reported outside the decision-making department would make the transaction more visible. In the payroll function, false payroll adjustment schemes can be identified. A periodic report identifying all employees receiving more than one payroll adjustment would reveal the scheme and deter the payroll clerk from committing the act.

Fraud Deterrence Procedures

Deterrence controls are designed to discourage individuals from committing fraud. The Control Environment section of the COSO model creates the environment for fraud deterrence.

A key control concept in fraud prevention is the concept of increasing the perception of detection. Convincing individuals that their scheme will be discovered might be the best fraud prevention strategy. The fear of detection is a psychological factor that causes people not to commit a fraud scheme. A fundamental tenet of fraud theory is that once pressures or rationalization exceeds the fear of detection, a person is more apt to commit the fraud scheme. Therefore, logic dictates that the higher the fear of detection, the higher the pressure and rationalization factor must be for fraud to occur.

Fraud Prosecution Procedures

Fraud prosecution controls is a new concept in the antifraud environment. The concept has evolved from the investigative process. In many instances, we know that a fraud has occurred and the losses are real. Unfortunately, because of how the control procedures are managed at the location, the investigators cannot identify exactly which person committed the act.

When analyzing the internal controls, focus should be on the likelihood of fraud occurring. If the fraud scheme occurs, can the fraud auditors establish, with a reasonable degree of certainty, which individual committed the fraud scheme? An audit trail allows for the documentation to re-create events or the management decision process.

Separation of duties allows for establishing accountability for the transaction, which correlates to fraud deterrence. The adequacy of documentation allows for proving accountability and proof that the fraud scheme occurred. The disciplinary measures ensure the internal controls operate in the manner intended by management.

Example

In one fraud case, a controller of a company was arrested for embezzling currency from the revenue cycle. At her trial, she was found not guilty. One reason for this verdict was that the firm's cash-handling procedures gave the opportunity for several different employees to steal the money. Specifically, in the sales and cash receipts business system, one of six individuals received cash receipts from customers, and all six had access to the cash drawer. At the end of the day, the funds were totaled and kept in the controller's office overnight. At least four individuals had keys to the controller office, including the two business owners. The sales work order system or the sales invoice system were not reconciled on a daily basis. With one of eight individuals having the opportunity to steal funds, the organization could not be successful in prosecuting the controller or anyone else.

The internal controls should have been designed to restrict each individual's access to the cash drawer. The funds should have been reconciled to the sales system. The money should have been counted, and the deposit slip prepared at the close of business each day. Clearly, this example shows that fraud prosecution controls are a key element to responding to fraud allegations.

IDENTIFIED FRAUD RISK CONTROL STRATEGY

The fraud risk assessment process starts with identifying the inherent fraud risk. Then, the internal controls are linked to the fraud risks. Due to the intentional effort to conceal the true nature of the transaction, most fraud risks often require a preventive and detective internal control. Auditors should follow this four-step process in developing a fraud control matrix:

1. Identify the inherent fraud scheme or the fraud scenario and the concealment strategies associated with the fraud scheme.

Exhibit 13.1 Internal Control for Front Companies/False Billing

Company Name
Matrix Fraud Internal Control Matrix
Risk Unit: Internal Control for Front Companies/False Billing

Control Opportunity	Preventive Control	Approval Control	Detective Controls	Deterrence/ Prosecution Controls	Fraud Risk Mitigation
Accounts payable	Separation of duty between invoice processing and vendor administration; Match purchase order and receiving report to invoice; New vendor registration procedures	Changes to master file report reviewed and approved daily; All invoices must be approved prior to payment; Accounts payable compares approval to authorized approver list	Monthly review of department responsibility statements; Review of changes to accounts payable master file changes	Fraud response policy; Annual audit of expenditures	Controls deemed adequate to prevent, detect, and deter fraud
Operating management	Operating management does not have access to input or process invoices for payment	Invoices over $25,000 require second approval	Comparisons of budget to actual by vice president and finance function	Fraud response policy; Annual audit of expenditures	Controls deemed adequate to prevent, detect, and deter fraud
Collusion: Accounts payable and operating management	None Collusion overrides preventive controls	Matching of required documents by accounts payable	None	Fraud response policy; Annual audit of expenditures	Fraud could occur with collusion; Rely on fraud deterrence

2. Link step one to the opportunity to commit the fraud scheme.

3. Link the fraud internal control strategies to the identified fraud risk.

4. There should be two conclusions:

   a. Is the fraud risk mitigation consistent with management's risk tolerance?

   b. If the fraud risk occurs, do we have the right fraud prosecution internal controls to successfully investigate the occurrence of the fraudulent event?

The internal fraud control matrix links the specific controls to the identified fraud risk. In preparing the matrix, identify the fraud risks at the inherent fraud risk level of the fraud scenario. Exhibit 13.1 illustrates the concept at the inherent fraud risk level.

14

Fraud Audit Report

The end result of a fraud audit is a document that provides the parties with information to make the necessary decisions. Management needs to know whether sufficient evidence exists to warrant an investigation. The fraud investigator and legal counsel need to understand what facts have been gathered to support the allegations. The fraud audit report should provide the basis for further action and the framework for an investigation. A fraud audit report written in the format of an expert witness report provides the medium to accomplish both the audit and the eventual legal objectives.

SUSPICIOUS TRANSACTION

A suspicious transaction is one that contains fraud indicators consistent with the fraud data profile, and the auditor is unable to conclude on the propriety of the transaction. As a result, the auditor recommends an investigation to refute the suspicion or gather additional evidence to support a referral to a prosecuting authority. Audit departments should have a protocol for reporting events versus an ad hoc process every time a fraud concern occurs in the audit process. A key part of the process is the written report of the event and the required actions.

The fraud audit report is the tool for documenting and communicating the auditor's suspicion. The audit standards issued by the professional audit organizations provide guidance to auditors on their responsibility to communicate concerns but not the format, style, and required content. The federal rules of evidence do, however, provide a model for developing the structure of a fraud audit report.

A fraud investigation report prepared by an expert witness is bound by the applicable rules of evidence. The end result of the investigation is the expert's written report. Within the federal court system, the expert must have an understanding of Rule 26, General Provisions Governing Discovery: Duty of Disclosure, found in the Federal Civil Procedure. The rule provides the minimum standards for what an expert's report should contain. The relevant section of Rule 26 related to expert's reports is reproduced next.

> **(2) DISCLOSURE OF EXPERT TESTIMONY. RULE 26(A) (2)**
> (A) In addition to the disclosures required by paragraph (1), a party shall disclose to other parties the identity of any person who may be used at trial to present evidence under Rules 702, 703, or 705 of the Federal Rules of Evidence.
> (B) Except as otherwise stipulated or directed by the court, this disclosure shall, with respect to a witness who is retained or specially employed to provide expert testimony in the case or whose duties as an employee of the party regularly involve giving expert testimony, be accompanied by a written report prepared and signed by the witness. The report shall contain a complete statement of all opinions to be expressed and the basis and reasons therefore; the data or other information considered by the witness in forming the opinions; any exhibits to be used as a summary of or support for the opinions; the qualifications of the witness, including a list of all publications authored by the witness within the preceding ten years; the compensation to be paid for the study and testimony; and a listing of any other cases in which the witness has testified as an expert at trial or by deposition within the preceding four years.
> (C) These disclosures shall be made at the times and in the sequence directed by the court. In the absence of other directions from the court or stipulation by the parties, the disclosures shall be made at least 90 days before the trial date or the date the case is to be ready for trial or, if the evidence is intended solely to contradict or rebut evidence on the same subject matter identified by another party under paragraph (2) (B), within 30 days after the disclosure made by the other party. The parties shall supplement these disclosures when required under subdivision (e) (1).

FRAUD AUDIT REPORT

Structuring the fraud audit report around the federal rules of evidence allows for a seamless transition from the audit standards to the investigation standards. The extent of compliance with the rules will depend on the facts and circumstances under which the auditor is operating. The fraud audit report consists of ten sections:

1. Background and assumptions
2. Statement of opinions
3. Relevant information
4. Exhibits
5. Factual background and assumptions
6. Recommended actions
7. Documents necessary to complete investigation
8. Document request
9. Compensation
10. Other report sections

Background and Assumptions

This section should contain who conducted the audit, the reason why the original audit was conducted, the report date, the date the audit was commenced, and the date of the opinions. The section may state, for example:

> The audit of accounts payable was conducted by the internal audit department as part of the regular audit schedule. The audit started on July 24, 2007. The opinions contained in this report are of September 8, 2007.

Statement of Opinions

In this section, the auditor describes the alleged fraud scheme by explaining the required elements of the fraud scheme. The auditor should use plain English to describe the fraud scheme. In a bribery scheme the report should offer an opinion on whether each required element of the scheme occurred or did not occur. For example:

> Was a contract issued to the vendor?
> Is there evidence of favoritism in awarding the contract?
> Who committed the act of favoritism?
> Is there evidence the perpetrator had knowledge of the favoritism?
> Is there evidence that the facts were concealed?
> Did the bribe influence the perpetrator?

The report should offer an opinion as to the creditability of each element as supported by the facts identified in the factual background and assumptions section of the report.

The opinions offered are based on the evidence available to the auditor at the time of the audit. The factual background and assumptions section describes the facts that support the auditor's opinions. The auditor's struggle in formulating an opinion will be over the sufficiency and competency of the evidence as related to the event. Is there sufficient and competent evidence to support the opinion in the report? The goal is not to determine guilt but rather whether credible evidence exists to suggest that an act has occurred and additional investigation is warranted.

The opinion would be written in this way:

> There is credible evidence to suggest that the fraud scheme (by each element of the scheme) is occurring.

or

> There is no credible evidence the fraud scheme is occurring.

In writing the opinion, the auditor should avoid:

- Using legal terminology beyond their expertise
- References to names of individuals and specific titles
- Specific opinions regarding malfeasance
- Opinions regarding guilt or innocence; that is for a judge or jury to decide

Relevant Information

This section indicates what documents, records, and other information the auditor relied upon to formulate his opinions. The auditor should identify the type of documents used to formulate their opinions. The report should include descriptions like: company reports, document names, relevant dates, account numbers, and other identifying information. It is generally not necessary to provide a listing of each specific document identified in the section, i.e., ABC Vendor invoice numbers 1000, 1001, etc. If the specific document is relevant to the case, it will be identified in the exhibits or the factual background and assumption section of the report.

Exhibits

This section provides a listing of the exhibits attached to the report. The exhibit provides sufficient explanation of each transaction supporting the finding. The first column of the exhibit should provide a reference to the document referenced in the exhibit. The remainder of the information on the exhibit should be sufficient to support the opinion and the facts stated in the factual background and assumptions section of the report.

Factual Background and Assumptions

The factual background and assumptions section, sometimes referred to as the basis of the auditor's opinion, must provide a clear statement of the facts supporting each opinion. The section should repeat each opinion and then provide a listing of the facts supporting the opinion. The basis for the auditor's opinion is derived from job responsibilities, company policies and procedures, performance of internal controls, facts, observations, and statements gathered during the audit. The facts stated will be derived from both direct evidence and circumstantial evidence.

Direct evidence tends to prove the fact by itself. No other evidence is necessary to establish the fact. Circumstantial evidence is all evidence of an indirect nature in which the event is deduced from the evidence by the process or probable reasoning either alone or with other collateral facts. A test used in weighting the value of the circumstantial evidence: Is it more probable that the event occurred based on the circumstantial evidence or more probable that the event did not occur? As with circumstantial evidence, no one piece of circumstantial evidence proves an event, like direct evidence, but rather the weight of the totality of the circumstantial evidence supports the opinion.

To illustrate the concept of direct and circumstantial evidence, let us use a revenue skimming case. Revenue skimming is the diversion of revenue prior to the recording of the sale. In this circumstance, we further assume that the perpetrator allegedly misappropriated both customer checks and currency from the revenue stream.

- **Direct evidence.** The customer service clerk is responsible for receiving all funds directly from a customer. The customer funds are handled only by the customer service clerk. Customers pay claims in currency, checks, and credit cards. Customer checks were deposited in the customer clerk's personal bank account.

- **Circumstantial evidence.** During the examination period, bank deposits were comprised solely of customer checks and credit cards. There was no evidence of currency on the bank deposit slips originating from the customer service function. The lack of currency by itself does not prove the theft; however, the lack of currency correlates to the theft of revenue.

Recommended Actions

The first action is to recommend an investigation or state that no additional audit work is necessary. When an investigation is deemed necessary, the audit report should indicate what additional records, documents, and/or witness statements are required to resolve the allegations. The additional evidence should be listed in the Documents Necessary to Complete the Investigation section under each stated opinion. As a matter of style, the Recommended Action section can be a stand alone section or included at the end of the audit opinion section.

If internal control weaknesses are observed, the internal control recommendations should be contained in a separate internal control report. The fraud audit report should reference the internal control report.

Documents Necessary to Complete Investigation

A listing of all the documents, records, or witness statements necessary to refute or support the fraud audit opinions. In the fraud audit report, this section identifies what records are necessary to perform the investigation. Often records, documents, and witnesses necessary to resolve allegations are not available to the auditor. These records are referred to as off-the-book records. In a vendor overbilling scheme involving kickbacks to the employee, for example, the necessary records to establish the kickback are at the vendor location or the employee's personal bank records. Without a comprehensive right to audit clause, auditors would be blocked from determining whether the vendor provided a kickback to an employee.

Document Request

A statement regarding which individual has been requested to provide the documents and any other actions necessary regarding the documents. A critical issue regarding documents external to the organization is always the authenticity of the documents. Legal counsel should be consulted regarding evidentiary matters regarding documents used in an investigation.

Compensation

Outside experts will have a statement regarding their financial arrangements to conduct the fraud audit. Internal auditors may not need this section.

Other Report Sections

Report Distribution Section   The report distribution section lists the parties receiving the report and states that the report expressly prohibits copying and further distribution of the report.

Limiting Condition Section   A limiting condition section states limitations or weaknesses relevant to the documents, access to records, or employees' failure to cooperate. It is hoped that all these issues are resolved prior to issuing a report. If they are not resolved, however, the failure to disclose the limitations could make the report misleading.

Attorney Work Product Statement   If the audit was conducted under the direction of legal counsel, the report should contain an attorney work product statement, which can be as simple as:

> Under the attorney work product rules, the report was prepared for attorney D.Q. Smith, Esq.

Confidentiality Statement   A confidentiality statement as to the information in the report should also be provided. A report should never be written assuming that a third party with adverse interests to the company will not read the report.

CONSIDERATIONS FOR FRAUD AUDIT REPORTS

The communication of the report is as critical as the facts supporting the report. The following will describe:

- Characteristics of good fraud audit reports
- Writing tips
- Other considerations

Characteristics of Good Fraud Audit Reports

- **Accuracy.** The three elements of accuracy are:

  1. **The facts are accurate.** There should be no errors in the facts. Facts are not arguable; only the interpretation or relatedness of the fact to the opinions should be debated.

  2. **The facts are complete.** The report should contain all the facts that are relevant to the case. The completeness of the facts should indicate all facts whether the facts are or are not supportive of the case.

  3. **The manner in which the facts are written is appropriate.** How the facts are stated in the report is just as important as their accuracy. Auditors should adhere to the adage "Check and then double check."

- **Bias.** Auditors should avoid using words that are biased or imply a bias.

- **Objectivity.** The writing style should be uninfluenced by emotion and personal opinion.

- **Timely.** "Timely" generally indicates that the report should be issued as quickly as possible. However, nothing is further from the truth in a fraud audit report. The measure of timeliness should be based on the necessary time to gather all the available facts in a complete and accurate manner.

- **Clarity.** Fraud cases tend to be complicated and involve an enormous amount of data and information. The job of auditors is to summarize the information in an easy-to-read format.

Writing Tips for Fraud Audit Reports

The writing style is as important as the actual facts of the report. The goal of the report is to communicate the issues in a clear and concise manner. In writing the fraud audit report, the author should:

- Avoid the use of absolute words (i.e., never).
- Avoid legal jargon. The key is to stay within your area of expertise.
- Avoid legal conclusions (i.e., committed fraud).
- Avoid words that hedge an opinion or statement of fact (i.e., appears).
- Avoid language that implies a bias (e.g., the manager behaved in an unethical manner).
- Avoid words that raise the standard unnecessarily (i.e., completely wrong).
- Avoid indirect reference words (i.e., pronouns, he or she).
- Avoid abbreviations.
- Use short and concise sentences and paragraphs. Write to communicate, not to impress.
- Proof the report and then proof it again.

Other Considerations

- Libel is when someone makes false statements regarding a person, the statements are communicated to a third party, and the person suffers damages from the communication. It is critical that the fraud audit report be factual as written and that the distribution of the report is limited to minimize the likelihood of damages to an individual's reputation.
- The report should avoid including written comments regarding an individual's personal life, even when the comments may be true. The report should focus on the individual's job duties or business dealings with the company.

- Documents should be contained in a separate binder as an attachment to the report, or the report should refer to the documents and advise readers that they are available and in the control of the auditor.

SAMPLE FRAUD AUDIT REPORT

The following is an illustrative example of a fraud audit report. The allegation is that a company manager perpetrated a false billing scheme using a front company.

I. Background and Assumptions   Joe Smith, Esq., counsel for Fraud Auditing Corp. in the matter of The ABC Company, has engaged Leonard W. Vona, CPA and CFE, to examine the Fraud Auditing Corp.'s documents and records for the direct purpose of offering opinions regarding the payments to The ABC Company.

I have prepared this report summarizing the opinions I have formulated from reviewing documents on July 24, 20X7. The documents were made available to me via the controller of Fraud Auditing Corp. I am qualified to issue such opinions based on my education, training, experience, and accreditations in such matters.

II. Statement of Opinions   My opinions are based on an independent examination of relevant materials provided by the controller and legal counsel of the Fraud Auditing Corp., independent research and investigation, authoritative treatises, and my past experience and professional knowledge in matters of this nature. The opinions contained in this report are as of October 31, 20X7.

Insofar as discovery is continued in this matter, I reserve the right to supplement or otherwise amend this report regarding factual assumptions, theories of fraud, and statements of opinions.

1. Credible evidence exists to suggest that the ABC Company is a front company.

2. Credible evidence exists to suggest that the services described on the ABC invoices were not provided to the Fraud Auditing Corp.

3. Credible evidence exists to suggest that internal employees either conspired to commit or committed the possible misappropriation of funds.

4. Credible evidence exists to suggest that person(s) involved knowingly converted Fraud Auditing Corp. funds for their own personal benefit.

5. Credible evidence exists to suggest that the Fraud Auditing Corp. has suffered a loss of $120,000.

The reasons, causes, and motives for these occurrences can be resolved with a thorough and complete investigation of the ABC Company's financial records and the personal financial records of identified internal employees.

III. Relevant Information   I have relied on the preceding facts and information to formulate my opinion contained in this report.

1. The ABC Company invoices, the supporting purchase orders, and purchase requisitions.

2. The Fraud Auditing Corp. general ledger and cash disbursement ledger for the 20X6 and 20X7 calendar year.

3. Copies of the front and back of Fraud Auditing Corp. canceled checks issued to the ABC Company.

4. Fraud Auditing Corp. personnel files.

5. Fraud Auditing Corp. purchasing and disbursement polices and procedures.

6. Interviews of Fraud Auditing Corp. employees.

IV. Exhibits
  Exhibit 1: Listing of payments to The ABC Company

  Exhibit 2: Copies of ABC Company invoices

  Exhibit 3: Copies, front and back, of Fraud Auditing Corp. canceled checks payable to The ABC Company

V. Factual Background and Assumptions
1. Credible evidence exists to suggest that The ABC Company is a front company.

   a. The ABC Company billing head indicates a mailing address of PO Box 934.

   b. The accounts payable function has no record of the physical address of The ABC Company.

   c. The telephone number listed on the invoice was answered by an answering service on three different occasions over a ten-day period. The ABC Company has not returned our messages.

   d. The manager who purported to engage The ABC Company was not aware of the physical location of The ABC Company.

   e. The incorporating documents for The ABC Company were filed by the XYZ Formation Company.

f. The Fraud Auditing Corp. checks were endorsed with a stamp that states "for deposit in Account Number 06041977."

2. Credible evidence exists to suggest that the services described on the ABC invoices were not provided.

   a. The ABC Company provided no reports detailing the work performed under its consulting agreement.

   b. The agreement between the Fraud Audit Corp. and The ABC Company is silent on providing a report summarizing results or recommendations.

   c. The Fraud Auditing Corp. manager who retained The ABC Company indicated that all meetings with The ABC Company occurred at the Fraud Auditing Corp offices.

   d. The Fraud Audit Corp. manager was unable to provide a list of other Fraud Auditing Corp. employees who were present at the meetings with The ABC Company.

   e. There were no entries on the Fraud Audit Corp. manager's calendar indicating meetings with The ABC Company.

   f. We were unable to identify any Fraud Audit Corp. employees who had a recollection of meeting with The ABC Company.

   g. The ABC Company invoices' description of services stated "Services Rendered."

3. Credible evidence exists to suggest that internal employees either conspired to commit or committed the misappropriation of funds.

   a. The hiring manager has stated he has no specific recollection of approving The ABC Company invoices.

   b. The approval signature purported to be that of the Fraud Audit Corp.'s manager is similar to other known writing samples of the Fraud Audit Corp.'s manager.

   c. The accounts payable function has no specific recollection of processing The ABC Company invoices for payment.

   d. The first payment date on the Fraud Auditing Corp.'s canceled check to The ABC Company occurred five days after the incorporation of the date of The ABC Company.

   e. The incorporation data was obtained from the Secretary of State's Web site.

4. Credible evidence exists to suggest that person(s) involved knowingly converted Fraud Auditing Corp. funds for their own personal benefit.

   a. The Fraud Audit Corp. manager is unable to provide any evidence that the services described on the vendor invoices were provided.

   b. The ABC Company is unwilling to respond to our inquiries regarding the investigation.

5. Credible evidence exists to suggest that the Fraud Auditing Corp. has suffered a loss of $120,000.

   a. As identified on Exhibit 1, there are 12 payments to The ABC Company totaling $120,000.

   b. Each payment was for $10,000.

VI. Documents Necessary to Determine that the ABC Company Is a Front Company

1. Documents submitted to the formation company to create the corporation.

2. Application for Creation of a Corporation used by the formation company to create The ABC Company.

3. Documents submitted to the formation company for payment of services rendered to The ABC Company.

4. The formation company telephone records for the month of creation and the month before and after the creation.

VII. Documents Necessary to Determine that Services Described on The ABC Invoices Were Not Provided to the Fraud Auditing Corp.

1. No additional documents are required.

2. A formal statement from the Fraud Auditing Corp. manager's recollection of the business relationship with The ABC Company.

VIII. Documents Necessary to Determine that Internal Employees Either Conspired to Commit or Committed the Misappropriation of Funds

1. No additional documents are required.

2. A handwriting expert should be considered to establish the authenticity of the approval signature on The ABC Company's invoices.

IX. Documents Necessary to Determine that Fraud Auditing Corp. has Suffered a Loss of $120,000

1. No additional records are required.

X. Documents Necessary to Determine that Person(s) Involved Knowingly Converted Fraud Auditing Corp. Funds for Their Own Personal Benefit

1. All ABC Company bank records of any and all accounts under signature authority of any of the named parties or entities, including but not limited to the known account numbers.

2. All personal bank records of any and all accounts under signature authority of any of the named parties or entities, including but not limited to the known account numbers.

3. All open or closed checking, savings, and money market accounts.

   a. Account opening documents including signature cards, copies of identification documents provided, and, if business account, copy of corporate resolution to open account and other business documents provided, which may include articles of incorporation for the business.

   b. Bank statements.

   c. Canceled checks (both sides).

   d. Deposit tickets and items (both sides of items, including ATM and direct deposits).

   e. ATM withdrawals.

   f. Credit and debit memos.

   g. Telephone transfer slips.

   h. Wire transfer records.

   i. Forms 1099 or backup withholding statements.

XI. Document Request General Counsel of the Fraud Auditing Corporation has been requested to obtain the documents requested in this report.

The bank providing the bank records of The ABC Company should provide a certification letter as to the authenticity of the bank records.

The examination of the requested documents could result in a further request for documents for an expanded period of time, either greater than the document request date or a more historical time frame.

XII. Compensation I am being compensated for my services in this matter at my firm's standard hourly rates for my work in analyzing the defendant's data and underlying documentation and for preparing this report.

XIII. Professional Background   My CV has been provided to the General Counsel of the Fraud Auditing Corp.

XIV. End of Report   Insofar as discovery is continued in this matter, I reserve the right to supplement or otherwise amend this report regarding factual assumptions, theories of fraud, and statements of opinions.

Respectfully submitted,
Leonard W. Vona, CPA & CFE

15

Fraud Investigation for the Auditor

This chapter provides auditors with guidance on how to respond to the risk of fraud. The first step is to understand the difference between auditing and investigation. The second step is to have the right policies to respond to the fraud risk. The last step is to provide the framework for preparing an investigation plan.

THE DIFFERENCES BETWEEN AUDIT AND INVESTIGATION

Understanding the difference between the auditing profession and the investigation profession is critical. While similar, audits and investigations are different. They have different bodies of knowledge and standards. Audits are based on auditing standards and accounting principles, policies, and procedures. Investigations are based on rules of evidence and criminal or civil procedure. For a criminal procedure, the violation is a matter of law and required burdens of proof. In civil actions, the issue concerns right and obligations of the contract resulting in potential tort action.

Fraud auditing is intended to identify transactions that have unresolved red flags of a fraud scheme. Management becomes the trier of fact. The fraud investigation is intended to refute or substantiate the allegation and provide evidence concerning the required acts of a law. The judge and jury becomes the trier of fact.

One of the first questions auditors conducting investigations ask should be: What is the objective of the investigation? In general, the objective is to resolve allegations of fraud. However, by understanding the end point of the case, auditors can better plan their investigation. Auditors should treat each case as if it is going to criminal court. In that way, they will follow the strictest procedures in the conduct of the investigation. Due to the realities of how organizations react to fraud allegations, pursuing the allegation to the fullest extent may not always be possible. If referral for criminal prosecution is not the plan, the decision should be a conscious one. The fraud audit should provide a seamless transition from the audit to the investigation. Ideally, the fraud audit report should become the fraud investigation report with minimal rewriting. The typical end points of the investigation are:

- Criminal prosecution
- Civil restitution
- Administrative resolution
- Clear innocent persons of suspicion
- Internal control improvement

ORGANIZATION POLICIES FOR RESPONDING TO FRAUD

There are two key policies for responding to the risk of fraud:

1. Suspicious transaction policy
2. Fraud response policy

Suspicious Transaction Policy

A critical question today is: When does the audit become an investigation? Starting the investigation too late may result in jeopardizing the collection of evidence, place parties on notice, and disclose information adverse to the organization. If the investigation is started too soon, however, the reputations of innocent parties may be adversely impacted.

Internal fraud investigations typically occur because of a reaction to an event. An allegation may have occurred through a hot line, accidental disclosure, and internal controls or through an audit finding. The response may be reactionary and emotional, based on the named parties to the fraud allegation. There may be a desire for the event to disappear or to visibly punish an individual. Due to the legal considerations surrounding fraud investigations, audit departments should develop a suspicious transaction policy. The intent of the policy is to provide a logical and unemotional response to fraud findings by auditors.

The elements of suspicious transaction policy are:

- **Define a suspicious transaction.** A suspicious transaction is any transaction identified in an audit that contains unresolved red flags associated with the fraud theory. The inherent assumption is that the audit department has established the red flag theory.

- **Understand the conversion cycle.** In many fraud schemes, the transfer of financial gain to the perpetrator is an off-the-books transaction. As a result, auditors do not have access to the necessary books and records to establish the knowingly converted aspect of the fraud. Auditors should document the likely conversion technique as part of the suspicious transaction theory. To illustrate: If the alleged scheme was an overbilling scheme, the contract manager would receive a kickback from the vendor for approving false charges on the invoice. The kickback is an off-the-books transaction.

- **Communicate to audit management.** The audit staff should communicate their findings using a secure and confidential communication medium. The communication should be limited to the chief auditor and the audit team.

- **Write the report.** The report should document facts and circumstances of the transactions. It should offer no legal opinions or suggestions of malfeasance.

- **Resolve a suspicious transaction through an investigation performed by an internal or external auditor in accordance with the fraud response policy.** The policy should require an investigation referral for all unresolved red flags.

- **Communicate to legal counsel.** The chief auditor should send the report directly and solely to legal counsel.

- **The legal department requests an investigation.** To request an investigation, the legal department sends a written request directly to the chief auditor or the fraud investigation team. In this way, issues such as attorney work product and privilege in context of a corporate investigation are protected before further evidence is gathered.

- **Secure legal advice on legal elements.** Counsel should be required to identify the legal issues and the elements of law that are in question or required to establish the violation of law in question.

- **Communicate with the audit committee.** The policy should indicate at what point the audit committee should be notified of a fraud investigation.

- **Audit committee approves the process.** The document should become an official policy of the audit department much like the internal audit charter.

- **Follow guidance.** Internal and external auditors should have written guidance on how to react to suspicious transactions identified in the course of an audit.

Fraud Response Policy

A properly written fraud response policy should anticipate questions and issues that arise when an allegation of fraud occurs. The policy should be written consistent with the culture of the organization and its international presence.

Management Responsibilities   The fraud response policy should provide an unequivocal statement concerning management's responsibility for preventing, detecting, and deterring fraud and the auditor's responsibility for responding to the risk of fraud. Ownership of fraud is the quiet debate between auditing and management. The policy statement should clarify roles and responsibilities.

A critical element of internal control theory is ensuring that organizational objectives are linked from the boardroom to the clerk. Policies and procedures must be linked with corporate objectives. Management, including audit management, must have clear and unequivocal responsibility for the managing the risk of fraud.

While the organization ethics policy addresses ethical behavior, the fraud response should reiterate the organization's zero tolerance for unethical behavior. The policy should communicate the organization's intention of investigating and prosecuting fraudulent matters to the fullest extent possible under administrative and legal procedures.

Fraud Investigation Team Authority and Responsibilities   The policy should identify the responsibilities of each team member. Ideally the team will be comprised of members of the audit, legal, human resources, public relations, and security departments. The purpose of the team is to provide a coordinated effort to assessing allegations of fraud and investigating fraudulent matters. The policy should provide for a central point to manage the fraud allegations, evaluate the creditability of the allegation, and plan the organization's response to the fraud incident. The policy should provide a statement regarding:

- The members of the fraud investigation team
- The responsibilities and the authority of the team regarding fraud matters
- The priority orders between the audit charter and the fraud investigation policy
- Access to company records, employees, and external parties

- The right to take possession of company records

- Reporting relationship to the audit committee

- Budgetary support for the investigatory process

What Is a Fraudulent Act?   The policy should distinguish between acts investigated under the policy and acts which are not consistent with the intent of the policy. Furthermore, acts which are administrative matters such as sick time abuse should be referred to the applicable management source.

The policy should use the fraud definition in the fraud risk assessment as the basis for determining which acts are under the purview of the policy. The goal is to provide employees guidance when to contact the fraud investigation team. The policy will require training and education regarding the fraud definition.

The fraudulent act section should identify specific exclusions to the section or contain a specific statement that no areas of fraud or illegal acts are excluded from the purview of the fraud investigation team. Typical exclusion considerations follow.

- An anticipated dollar minimum to investigate the fraudulent matter.

- Illegal acts committed by the corporation. These acts may be better investigated under the charge of the board audit committee.

- Areas of the enterprise-wide risk assessment that are beyond the practical experience of the investigation team.

On face, this section seems fairly straightforward. However, it requires the greatest extent of consideration and deliberation within the organization. At some point there will be debate as to whether an event is under the purview of the investigation team. Still, anticipating or defining the scope of a fraudulent act is difficult. Policy statements have used short definitions to exhaustive listings of fraudulent acts to provide guidance. This section should refer questions of statement applicability to the chair of the fraud investigation team.

What Constitutes a Reportable Incident?   Allegations of fraud will primarily occur from the:

- **Organization's ethics hot line.** The policy should address who is responsible for assessing allegations and at what point the fraud investigation team should be notified of the allegation.

- **Fraud audit reports.** Logically, all completed fraud audit reports will be forwarded to the fraud investigation team. The policy should link to the audit suspicious transaction policy.

- **Management observation.** The important aspect is at what point management should communicate its concerns or observations. The statement should advise management to report both suspected and actual incidents of fraudulent acts. Ideally, management should not investigate fraud or confront employees regarding fraudulent acts. However, the geographic spread of the organization's facilities will impact the reality of management's involvement in the investigation process.

Procedure for Reporting Incident for Investigation   Procedures for reporting an incident should address:

- **Communication medium.** The statement should provide a preferred method of communicating allegations of fraud. There are pros and cons of both verbal and written communication. The corporation's legal counsel should be consulted on this aspect.

- **Timeliness of reporting the incident.** The statement should include a time requirement to report concerns. Organizations have used two approaches: a qualitative standard "without delay" or a quantitative approach "within 24 hours."

- **Confidentiality of the allegation.** Both the suspect and the person reporting the allegation need to be protected to avoid damaging the reputations of innocent parties. The statement should provide clear and unequivocal guidance regarding confidentiality and the impact of disclosing information.

- **Suspect party.** There is balance between the needs of the investigative process and the rights of the suspect party to be notified of the investigation. The policy should provide guidance on when, who, and how the suspect is notified.

Procedure for Responding to Allegation   The first step is to determine whether the allegation is credible. If the allegation is not credible, the reasons for not performing the investigation should be documented. The second step is to investigate all credible allegations. The investigation process is intended to document the facts and circumstances of the allegation. The policy should indicate the need for prompt action to investigate and resolve allegations of fraud.

Internal Investigation: Identify Responsibility to Investigate   Unfortunately, fraud is committed at all levels of the organization—employees, fraud investigation team, senior management, and board members. Due to political realities of conducting investigations at higher levels of the organization, the policy should differentiate between the responsibilities of the investigation team and the audit committee to investigate fraudulent matters.

Internal Reporting: Communication Process   The policy should identify time points at which fraud allegations, fraud investigations, and fraud reports are communicated to senior management, the audit committee, outside accountants, and regulators. The committee should not bear the burden of these decisions; rather the policy should clearly state the time schedule.

Communication with the suspected party is also important to consider. The when, who, and how of communicating the fraud allegation to the suspected party is an important policy decision. Clearly, there are competing interests in informing the perpetrator. Global customs, corporate cultures, employee rights, legal considerations, and investigation requirements will impact the decision. The organization should provide guidance on this delicate subject.

Coordination with Law Enforcement   The criminal prosecution of illegal acts requires the assistance of law enforcement and applicable prosecuting authorities. The statement should address which team member has the responsibility to communicate the illegal act and when the communication should occur.

Prosecution Policy   Referring individuals to law enforcement becomes both a business decision and an emotional issue. The prosecution statement should state the organization's policy for referring individuals to a prosecuting attorney. If the decision making is not a simple yes or no, the decision making process in deciding to refer or not refer should be clearly stated in the prosecution section.

In those cases where the individual is not referred, the decision should be communicated to the audit committee along with the reasons for the lack of referral action.

Legal Determinations   Fraud is a legal matter. The policy should have a simple and direct statement regarding the general counsel's responsibility to provide timely support to the fraud investigation team.

Employee Termination Policy   The process for suspending, terminating, or reprimanding employees alleged to be involved in fraudulent matters needs to be defined. Remember, until a court of law finds the individual guilty, the person is only alleged to have committed an act. Due to the various legal considerations involving employee rights or wrongful termination, the role of human resources in the decision-making process should be clearly identified.

Protections   Fear of reprisal is a reason that people often state for not reporting crimes. The company should not tolerate harassment or adverse consequences to employees, customers, or vendors that report incidents. Also, the policy should state that the company will not tolerate employees, customers, or vendors that report false allegations with a malicious intent.

Financial Recovery Policy   The policy of the organization should be to attempt to recover all lost funds from the perpetrator of a fraud. A second aspect is the appropriate actions to prevent further loss until the investigation is completed.

Public Relations   Fraud can be a popular topic for the newspaper. The key is to ensure that the public relations function is aware of the fraud allegation and that a clear point person is selected for handling inquires regarding these matters.

Administration   The document should indicate the owner of the policy and his or her responsibility to update the policy on a periodic basis, not to exceed two years.

Confidentiality and Discretion   The policy should state that all communications, either verbal or written, should be kept strictly confidential without exception. The policy should provide guidance to:

- Fraud investigation team
- Operating management in the department impacted by the fraud
- Senior management
- Board audit committee

Distribution of reports beyond the distribution list or verbal communication of the alleged act is grounds for termination.

Approval of Policy   The policy should be approved at the highest level within the organization, preferably by the chair of the board, chair of the audit committee, and the chief executive officer.

FRAMEWORK FOR PREPARING AN INVESTIGATION PLAN

A fraud investigation methodology should follow a logical progression for resolving allegations of fraud. The process starts in a general fashion and moves to the specifics. The process continually gathers documentary evidence and witness statements that are designed to allow the investigator to write a report and offer opinions regarding the alleged act.

At each step of the investigation, careful attention is given to the acquisition, preservation, and analysis of evidence. The investigation follows both a linear and a circular approach. It is important to follow a logical progression in performing the investigation. However, it is equally important to continually reevaluate the evidence and the case theory.

The fraud investigation methodology utilizes nine steps:

1. Develop preliminary fraud theory.

2. Develop the fraud audit program.

    a. Understand the mechanics of fraud schemes.

    b. Identify the legal elements of the crime.

    c. Identify necessary evidence by legal element.

3. Perform document examination.

    a. Gather the evidence.

    b. Preserve the evidence to avoid chain of custody issues.

    c. Analyze the evidence in regard to the fraud theory.

4. Link evidence to witnesses.

5. Revaluate the fraud theory.

6. Perform interviews.

    a. Identify witnesses.

    b. Determine the order of interviews.

    c. Determine the purpose of the interviews.

7. Revaluate the fraud theory.

8. Conclude the investigation.

9. Write the report.

The remainder of the chapter will discuss developing the preliminary fraud theory. Steps two through nine are beyond the purview of this book.

DEVELOP THE PRELIMINARY FRAUD THEORY

The development of the fraud theory is intended to assist in resolving allegations of fraud. The investigator will develop a theory on how the fraud occurred, the parties involved in the fraud, and the time frame during which the fraud occurred. The theory becomes the basis for developing an investigation plan for examining documents and interviewing witnesses. Since the fraud theory is based on a series of assumptions, the theory should be continually challenged throughout the investigation process as to parties involved and the basis for the allegations. The investigator should focus on whether the evidence refutes or supports the fraud theory. These questions should be raised in developing the fraud investigation plan:

- **What is the fundamental fraud scheme?** Every business system has inherent fraud schemes that represent the majority of frauds in the system. The fraud scheme has typical characteristics that allow investigators to plan how to conduct the investigation.

- **What is the crime?** Each crime has what is referred to as elements of proof or the required acts of the crime. This consists, in essence, of the evidence the law requires the investigator to gather and present. The fraud scenario and the crime should be linked together.

- **How is the fraud concealed?** Each fraud scheme has standard ways of concealment of fraud. By focusing the data analysis and the audit procedure on the concealment strategy, the fraud will become apparent to the investigator. The concealment strategy will also help to illustrate the intent of the perpetrators.

- **Who in the organization may be involved?** The scheme will direct the investigator to the department in which fraud is occurring. Is one individual, a group of employees, or a group of employees and management committing the fraud? This assessment will impact which documents are examined, the order of interviewing witnesses, and how to link the evidence to the specific statute.

- **Who outside of the organization may be involved?** Are vendors or customers involved? Is there an external individual attempting to perpetrate the crime?

- **How sophisticated are the parties who are committing the crime?** Is this crime perpetrated by a first-time offender, a repeat offender, or a member of an organized crime group? There is typically a correlation between the perpetrator's experience and the sophistication of the fraud.

- **What stage is the fraud in?** That is, how long has the fraud been occurring? This question will provide the investigator with guidance on the resources necessary to conduct the investigation and the magnitude of the losses.

- **How did we become aware of the fraud?** The greater the common knowledge of the fraudulent act, the greater the opportunity for evidence to be missing or damaged, for witness tampering, and for concern about the safety of the investigator.

- **Why did the fraud occur?** Did the fraud occur due to an internal control breakdown, management override, or extortion? The investigation team should identify and understand the cause for the fraud.

- **What documents, records, and witnesses are available?** Evidence is the critical issue in resolving allegations of fraud. The investigator should perform a preliminary inventory of available evidence. The inventory should be a written document.

- **What state are the records in? Do you have original or copies of records?** The relevance and weight of the evidence will correlate to the eventual burden factor of convincing management or proceeding with a legal action.

- **Are all the necessary records under the control of your client? When the investigator has direct access to the records, documents, and witnesses, this is referred to as "on the books."** If the records are "on the books," the investigator can operate in a covert manner for confidentiality purposes and should be able to resolve the allegations. "Off the books" is when the investigator does not have direct access to the records, documents, and witnesses. If the records are off the book, eventually it will be necessary to make the investigation more public, and legal action may be necessary to obtain the necessary records.

- **How often did the fraud occur?** The frequency of the fraud will assist in proving intent, the scope of the examination, and the investigator's ability to find the fraudulent transactions.

- **What is the dollar range of the damages?** The economic damages will correlate to the viability of a civil action and eventual criminal charges.

- **How does the perpetrator obtain the financial gain?** Is the transfer on the books or off the books? Was the gain an economic gratuity, currency, or a wire transfer? How **sophisticated** were the concealment strategies used to conceal the conversion of funds to the perpetrator?

- **How will you prove intent?** Intent may not be necessary in a civil case. This issue should be clearly discussed with counsel. The intent factor will link to the identified concealment strategies.

- **How do you calculate damages?** Is the loss calculation based on direct evidence, circumstantial evidence, or an economic loss calculation?

- **Will the case be built on direct or circumstantial evidence?** The type of evidence will impact the approach to building your case. Direct evidence tends to illustrate the fraudulent act by itself. Circumstantial evidence tends to require the gathering of multiple sources of evidence to illustrate the fraudulent act.

- **What are the legal defenses to the allegations?** Discuss this point with counsel. The defenses will vary by the action and facts and circumstances of the case. The perpetrator will also raise defenses to the fraud allegation. Anticipating the defenses allows for a better-planned investigation.

- **How do the documents link to the perpetrators?** The documents have to be relevant to the fraudulent act and the perpetrator. The investigator must show either a direct or a circumstantial link between the evidence and the perpetrator.

- **Are there witnesses who can corroborate the fraudulent action?** Here the investigator begins the process of identifying internal and external parties who would have knowledge of the alleged act.

- **How overt will the investigation be?** In the early stages of an investigation, there may be reasons to maintain confidentiality. Company management may wish to avoid publicity. The investigator needs to assess what impact this will have on the conduct of investigatory procedures.

The end result of the planning process is an investigative plan that allows auditors to perform a complete, proper investigation. Just as a strong foundation is the key to building a house, a strong investigation plan becomes the foundation for conducting an investigation.

Index

AICPA. *See* American Institute of Certified Public Accountants

ATM. *See* Awareness, Theory, and Methodology

Agents, 84–85, 126–128, 131, 158

American Institute of Certified Public Accountants, 6, 20, 45

Assumptions, 42, 65–66, 125, 132, 135, 179–181, 185–186, 190, 193, 200

Attorney Work Product Statement, 36, 84, 183, 193, 197

Audit:
  committee, 39–40, 46–47, 101, 193, 195, 197–198
  definition, 121–122
  plans, 1, 26, 28–29, 36, 63, 70, 99, 107
  procedures, 2–4, 17, 33, 35–37, 40, 51–59, 64–67, 70, 94, 96, 98, 100, 112, 151–152, 158, 168, 200
  process, 2, 7–8, 16, 19, 23, 36, 55–56, 63, 107–108, 119, 122–126, 177
  response, 13, 19–21, 23, 25, 27, 29, 31, 33, 35, 57, 67, 94, 100, 105, 158, 171–172, 175, 192–194
  standards, 2, 20, 152, 170, 177–178, 191, 196
  strategy, 32, 111–116, 146–148

Awareness, 3–4, 13, 21, 28–29, 46–47, 52, 56, 59, 126, 171

Awareness, Theory, and Methodology, 3–5, 7, 9, 11, 13, 15

Background checks, 115, 141

Bias, 2, 14, 20, 27, 32, 75, 80, 183–184

Bid rigging schemes, 22. *See also* Vendor(s)

Bids, 22, 26, 122, 124–134, 173

Block sample, 138

Bribery, 11, 31, 179

Bribery schemes:
  advanced communication, 126, 128
  bid avoidance, 126–127
  false statements in, 126–128
  key control points, 126, 129–132
  management overrides, 126–128

Business systems, 1–2, 9–10, 12, 14, 27–28, 31, 36–37, 40, 44–46, 50–51, 55, 57–58, 60, 172, 174, 200

COSO. *See* Committee of
    Sponsoring Organizations
Checks:
    accounts payable, 99
    bank, 72, 85–86
    cancelled, 106, 186, 189
    company, 16
    convert to cash, 125
    counterfeit, 102
    customer, 157–158, 160–161,
        163, 181
    distribution, 73
    endorsements, 16, 34, 104–106,
        146, 148
    flip-flopping, 104
    interception scheme, 104
    number, 72, 90
    payroll, 28, 31, 34, 67, 145–146,
        148, 150–151, 153
    refund, 105
    requested, 58, 61
    returned, 102
    tampering schemes, 103–104
    theft of, 102–103, 105
Circumstantial evidence, 135,
    181, 201
Civil restitution, 192
Code of ethics, 40
Collusion, 15, 34, 93, 102, 112, 145,
    147, 151, 159–160, 163, 175
    in schemes, 169
    logical, 11, 13–14, 31, 65, 89,
        173
Committee of Sponsoring
    Organizations, 51, 170,
    172–173
Concealment, 3, 5, 10, 13–14, 52,
    63–64, 66–68, 87–88, 95, 100,
    155, 166–167, 169, 200
Concealment Strategies:
    before recording sales, 157–158
    business-specific, 15
    complexity, 16
    corresponding audit procedures,
        27, 56

currency substitution, 160
data analysis routines, 77
defined, 14
disguised purchases, 99
embezzlement, 160
employee reimbursed, 102
favored vendor, 26
generic, 15
identify, 15
investigation plan, 200
magnitude, 64
overbilling, 93
red flags, 10, 13, 26, 32, 63, 73
simple, 63
sophistication of, 4, 63–64, 75–76
theft, 166
transactions, 58
unique, 10
Conclusions, 16, 79, 96, 135,
    176, 184
Conduct, 40, 46, 49, 61, 171
Confidentiality statement, 183
Conflict of interest, 40, 73, 120, 162
    in schemes, 94, 97
Contract schemes:
    cost mischarging. *See* Mischarging
    defective pricing, 110–111
    nonconforming materials or serv-
        ices, 110–111
    overbilling, 116–118
    progress payment, 110–111
Control:
    access, 23, 56, 77, 126–127,
        129–130, 132, 162, 169
    environment, 28, 38, 46, 58, 124,
        166–167, 169–171
    identification, 21
    numbers, 22, 25, 72
    risk, 3
    theory, 11, 28–30, 169–170, 172
Corruption, 6, 43, 119–120, 125
    in schemes, 11, 41
Credit cards, 16–17, 58, 85, 99,
    103, 124, 139–142, 157–158,
    160–162, 181

Crime, 12, 120, 159, 198–200
Criminal, 11, 33, 49, 84, 109, 119,
    191–192, 197, 201

Data:
  codes, 23, 72, 98, 131, 141–142,
    147
  dictionary, 71–72
  homogeneous groups, 72, 77,
    119–120, 195, 197
  integrity analysis, 71–72, 74–75
  mapping, 69, 71–73
  profile, 10–11, 14, 21, 27, 31–32,
    36, 56, 69–73, 76, 79, 161,
    172, 177
  tables, 71–72
Database(s), 32, 69, 71–75, 78,
    80, 86, 96, 113, 146–147,
    151–153
Deposits, 34, 62, 145–146, 150,
    155–156, 158, 160, 174, 181,
    187, 189
Document(s):
  billing, 107
  condition of, 22, 24, 62, 91
  contract, 107
  copies, 91
  created, 62
  data on, 22
  examination of, 32–33, 101, 115,
    151, 199–200
  experts, 62
  falsified, 33–34, 55, 85, 112, 127,
    154, 160, 170
  filed, 85
  files, 22
  fraudulent, 62
  handwritten, 25
  incorporating, 186
  missing, 34, 91–92, 112
  necessary, 84, 179, 182, 188
  original, 63, 112–113
  reference, 108
  requested, 179, 182, 188
  scanning of, 62

  shipping, 98, 100, 113
  source, 99, 153
  submitted, 188
Documentary evidence, 198
Documentation:
  bid, 133–134
  false, 15, 61, 105, 122, 166
Drill down, 56–57
Duplicate information, 25, 35,
    72–75, 77, 80, 90, 92, 117,
    138, 140, 146, 150

Economic model, 32
Economic substance, 23, 32–33
Embezzlement, 16, 34–35, 42, 44,
    50, 56, 65, 68, 157, 159–161,
    163, 166
  after initial recording of
    sales, 159
  cash receipts from nonrevenue
    sources, 159–160
  currency substitution, 160
  customer blow-out, 163
  delinquent customer, 163
  favored terms, 162
  front customer, 161–162
  lapping, 160–161
  refunds, 163
  resale of product, 161
  revenue skimming, 158–159
  theft of payments, 163
Employee involved schemes:
  false, 34
  family member, 148
  fictitious, 116, 145–147, 150
  ghost employee, 28, 31–32,
    34–35, 36, 145–157. See also
    Red flags
  no-show, 28, 116, 147
  pre-employment, 146–147
  temporary, 147–148
  terminated, 146
Errors, 6, 16, 19, 22–23, 25, 27–28,
    32, 39, 52, 57, 75, 110–111,
    117–118, 124, 134, 141, 183

Event(s):
  combination of, 91
  company, 99
  consequential, 48
  converting to financial
    gain, 53
  correlated to, 158
  description of, 139
  evidence, 180–181
  external, 85
  feasibility, 53
  fraudulent, 3
  in scoring examples, 49–50
  inconsequential, 48
  investigation of, 195
  linking with patterns, 23
  measurable, 46
  morale, 46–47
  observed, 26, 91
  past, 123
  pressures, 7
  probability of occurring, 52
  reaction to, 192
  re-create, 174
  red flag, 13, 142
  reporting on, 177
  tickets, 17
  time, 67, 139
  travel, 140–141
  triggering, 13, 26
  type of, 22
  unpredictable, 38
Evidence:
  additional, 177
  admissible, 33
  audit, 33
  circumstantial, 135, 181, 201
  collection of, 27–28, 33, 36,
    124, 193
  consideration, 33
  credible, 36, 180, 185–188
  direct, 20, 181, 201
  event. See Event(s)
  eliminate, 62
  indirect, 20, 28

  information, 106
  intent of, 115
  internal controls. See Internal
    control(s)
  known, 28
  observed, 21. See also Internal
    control(s)
  obtained, 33
  providing, 28, 191
  specific, 22
  stored, 33
  sufficient, 26, 180, 185–188
  tampering, 105
  work performance, 146–148,
    150–151
Exclusion and Inclusion Theory, 69,
    71, 73, 79
Expenditure cycle, 157
Expenditure schemes:
  accounts payable, 102
  cash disbursement, 83
  check tampering. See Checks
  disguised purchases. See Purchase
    schemes
  diversion of payment, 99
  employee reimbursement, 102
  false billing. See False billing
    schemes
  money laundering, 84
  pass-through, 84, 97–98
  procurement cards. See
    Procurement cards
Expense avoidance, 41
Expert testimony, 178
Extortion, 41, 43, 120, 125, 201

False billing, 22–23, 44, 58, 75,
    78, 80, 84, 86–88, 91, 93–94,
    96–97, 125, 135, 175, 185
False positives, 71, 74
False statements, 95, 126–127, 131,
    158, 184
Fictitious:
  bids, 127
  charges, 112, 166

companies, 59, 79, 85, 102, 127. *See also* Red flags

customer, 45

employee. *See* Employee involved schemes

materials, 117–118

receipt, 141

reports, 116–117

vendors. *See* Vendor(s)

Filtering criteria, 73, 76

Financial reporting, 40–42, 4, 50, 186. *See also* Internal control(s)

Financial statements, 2, 6, 39–40, 42, 55, 76, 115

Fraudulent act, 8, 13, 16, 55, 60, 65, 109

Fraud:

audit report, 177–185, 192, 195

circle, 10

computer, 42

conversion, 4, 10, 12–13, 16, 53, 87–88, 91, 93–95, 98–99, 102, 142, 145, 151, 158, 167, 193, 201

definition, 4–6, 41–42, 45–46, 120, 195

information, 42

likelihood, 8–9, 13, 41, 46–47, 55, 61, 70, 87, 90, 112–113, 167, 172, 174, 184

likelihood score, 41, 47

magnitude, 32, 57, 63–64, 66, 76, 78, 89, 94, 145, 200

prevention, 5–6, 12, 38–40, 48, 51–52, 60–65, 99, 103, 119, 137, 169–175, 194, 198

prosecution, 6, 173–176, 192, 197

response, 10–11, 20–23, 25, 27, 29, 31, 33, 35–36, 57, 66–67, 94, 100, 105, 158, 171–172, 175, 192–194

risk control procedure, 8, 11, 13, 15, 38, 46, 51–52, 65, 87, 100

scenario, 9–10, 13–14, 21, 26–28, 34, 52, 56–57, 65–66, 68, 70, 87–88, 95, 111, 174, 176, 200

sophistication, 4–5, 11, 14, 57, 63–65, 75–76, 78, 86, 200–201

triangle, 4, 7–8, 29, 41, 46, 51, 60

variations, 10, 12–13, 26, 51, 56, 58–59, 85–86, 89, 91, 98, 109–111, 114, 126, 145, 151, 158, 160–161

Front companies, 14, 23, 83–87, 89–91, 97–98, 100, 125, 175, 185–186, 188

Generally Accepted Accounting Principles (GAAP), 2, 42

General ledger, 56–58, 62, 72–73, 78–79, 93, 98, 103, 148, 153, 186

Global risk, 7, 18, 50, 56, 65

Government regulation avoidance, 41

Gratuity, 120

Gross magnitude risk calculation, 48

Handwriting, 33–34, 63, 68, 95, 105, 139–141, 146, 157, 188

Hot line, 21, 38, 46, 161, 192, 195

Illegal acts, 6, 16, 40, 43, 45–46, 83–84

Independent data comparison, 32–33

Industry variation, 10, 13

Inherent fraud risk, 9, 10–13, 26–29, 39, 51–52, 70, 108, 110–111, 145, 157, 170, 172, 174, 176, 193, 200

Inhibitors, 11, 28–30, 63–64, 78, 89, 169, 171

Innovative schemes, 155

Intent factor, 109, 135

Internal Control(s):
  assessment, 27, 56, 60
  audit procedures, 32, 51, 65,
    171–172
  changes to, 16
  considerations, 57
  cost, 170
  design of, 21, 57, 79, 174
  effectiveness, 1, 11–12, 20, 37,
    40, 47–48, 52, 64–65, 75, 78,
    174, 181
  evidence, 33
  financial reporting, 40
  identified, 60–61
  improvement of, 192
  intuitive factors, 29
  linked to risk, 4, 37–38, 55, 170,
    174, 176
  management, 169–171
  model, 51
  monitoring, 21
  observable events, 22
  opportunity. *See* Opportunity
  override, 29
  ownership, 29, 56, 60
  payroll, 152
  prior audit results, 110
  risk tolerance, 39
  sampling and, 20
  testing of, 1–2, 20–21
  theory, 29, 194
  transactions, 31, 57–58, 192
  weakness of, 12, 19, 93,
    182, 201
Interviews, 32, 52, 66–67, 69,
  80–81, 94, 96, 98, 101,
  112–115, 123, 147, 149,
  151–152, 186, 199–200
Investigation, 4, 6, 16, 19–20, 26,
  36, 91, 103, 119, 123–124,
  137, 153, 177–182, 185–186,
  188, 191–202

Judgment, 29, 69–70, 73–74, 120,
  135

Kickback schemes, 4, 31, 97, 124,
  127, 193

Legal counsel, 109, 116, 122–123,
  135, 177, 182–183, 185, 193
Legal definition, 5–6, 121–122
Libel, 184
Logic testing, 32, 77, 80, 101

Macro-risk level, 38
Mapping. *See* Data
Materiality, 76, 137
Mega-risk level, 38
Micro-risk level, 38
Misappropriation involved
  schemes, 6, 41, 44, 52, 65, 68,
    83, 96, 100
Mischarging schemes:
  costs, 111
  false interpretation, 115
  false or fictitious, 112
  increased rates, 114
  intention errors, 111
  layering, 114–115
  multiple contracts, 113
  no benefit, 116
  overstatement, 112
  prior purchase, 113
Misuse, 17, 42, 99, 101, 165, 167.
  See also Payroll schemes
Mitigation, 38–39, 175–176
Monitoring, 21, 38, 40, 99,
  170–173. *See also* Internal
  control(s)

Net risk loss calculation, 48
Nonperformance, 11, 22, 30, 65,
  87, 100, 170

Opportunity:
  control, 2, 13, 56, 78, 87–88,
    124, 169
  created, 99
  fraud, 11, 51–52, 56–57, 59, 70,
    152, 159, 165

pressures and rationalization, 29, 46
profit, 108
time card, 152
to commit fraud, 8–9, 11–13, 26, 29, 60, 67, 176
to steal, 174
Overbilling, 23, 59, 75, 78–79, 93–97, 100, 107, 109, 111–112, 114, 135, 193
concealment strategies. *See* Concealment strategies
in contracts. *See* Contract schemes
red flags. *See* Red flags
schemes, 15, 93, 97, 107, 109, 116–117, 182, 193
Override(s), 14–15, 20, 52, 64–65, 89–90, 95, 100, 124, 169, 171, 175, 201
internal control. *See* Internal control(s)
involved in schemes, 42, 129–132, 170
management. *See* Bribery schemes
Overtime, 31, 45, 65–68, 76, 151–152
Ownership, 16, 29, 38, 42, 50, 56, 60, 84, 94, 97, 101, 128, 133, 194. *See also* Internal control(s)

PCAOB. *See* Public Company Accounting Oversight Board
Passive approach, 1, 17, 19, 21
Pass-through company schemes, 23. *See also* Expenditure schemes
Patterns:
data, 69–70, 76–77, 79, 80, 123, 126, 138, 142, 159
invoices, 87
red flags, 56, 132
reported hours, 68
transaction. *See* Transaction(s)
types, 23

Payroll schemes:
bonus, 154
commissions, 154
false adjustment, 173
false customer benefits, 155
false customer credits, 155
fictitious year-end sales, 155
fringe benefits, 154
misuse, 154
overtime, 31, 45, 76, 151–152
payroll calculation 145, 153–154
payroll tax deposits, 156
quota changing, 155
sale of promotional items, 155
unclaimed checks, 148
using ghost employees. *See* Ghost employee
Perspective:
audit, 40, 53, 73, 119, 121–122, 158
auditor's, 37, 39
criminal's, 84
legal, 33, 19–120
management's, 39
organization, 39
Pressures, 7–8, 12, 14, 29, 46–47, 169, 173
Price, 26, 93, 108, 110–111, 115, 117, 120, 125, 127–135, 140–141, 161–12, 165, 168
Proactive approach, 17, 19, 27, 36
Procurement, 26, 81, 99, 119, 122, 126
cards, 9, 64, 72, 99, 140
schemes, 99
Prosecution, 173–176, 177, 192, 197
Public Company Accounting Oversight Board, 1, 40, 48
Public relations, 194, 198
Purchase schemes, 98, 113, 175, 186

Rationalization, 7–8, 11–12, 14, 29, 46–47, 169, 173
Reactive approach, 19, 21, 60

Real estate schemes, 97
Receipts, 30, 42, 102, 113, 115,
    124, 137–143, 157, 159–160,
    166, 174
Records:
    off-the-books schemes, 33, 193
    on-the-books schemes, 33
Red flags:
    bids, 22, 131–134
    concealment, 26, 34, 68, 87–88,
        95, 100
    fictitious company, 22
    ghost employee, 150
    of fraud, 1–4, 10, 13, 19–21, 32,
        33, 35, 57, 96, 119, 125, 191
    of lapping, 161
    overbilling, 109
    potential for, 162
    theory, 133, 173, 193
    to identify, 126, 172
    travel, 139–140, 142–143
    unresolved, 193
    vendor invoices, 24
Related parties, 16, 40, 115. *See also*
    Transaction(s)
Relevant information, 120,
    179–180, 186
Revenue:
    obtained improperly, 45
    skimming, 83
Risk assessment:
    business-process, 18, 38–39,
        50–53, 56
    enterprise-wide, 9, 18, 38, 41–42,
        46, 50, 56, 195
    fraud, 2–5, 9–14, 18, 20–21, 28,
        37–41, 44–46, 51, 55–57, 70,
        80, 83, 108, 137, 157,
        170–172, 174, 195
    fraud penetration, 18, 38, 44–45,
        51, 55–59, 64–65, 76–78
    organizational, 37

SAS. *See* Statement of Auditing
    Standards
Sample. *See* Block sample

Sampling, 2–4, 13–14, 32, 35, 56,
    69, 71, 75, 96, 158. *See also*
    Transaction(s) and Internal
    control(s)
Sampling procedure, 20, 27,
    69–60
Sarbanes-Oxley, 1
Search routines, 69, 71–72, 75–76
Separation of duties, 29–31, 60, 65,
    160, 172, 174–175
Signatures, 22, 30, 61–63, 67–68,
    84, 104–105, 187–189
Small business schemes, 105
Statement of Auditing Standards,
    6, 170
Statement of opinions, 179, 185
Statues, 119–121

Theft, 16–17, 40, 42–43, 60, 99,
    102–105, 148, 155, 157–161,
    163, 165–167, 181
Theft schemes:
    asset purchase, 168
    asset retirement, 168
    assets, 165–167
    excessive expenditure, 168
    no business use, 167
Timing, 23, 37, 40, 55
Tips, 1, 14–15, 38, 97, 161
Transaction(s):
    altered, 159
    analysis, 13, 57
    arm's length, 135
    assumptions, 66
    booked, 125, 193
    business, 11, 14, 17, 19, 27, 30,
        32, 65, 70, 107, 173
    codes, 72
    concealing, 16
    considerations, 63
    core business, 38, 55
    examine, 36
    excluding, 70–71, 73
    fraudulent, 4, 13–14, 20–21, 31,
        33, 36, 38, 59, 63–64, 70, 75,
        77–78, 81, 83, 145, 161, 201

identify, 21, 56, 70, 72, 74,
    172, 191
including, 70, 73
investigate, 36
known, 14
layered, 114
missing, 77
organizational, 69
pattern(s), 32, 69
payroll, 145
population of, 57–58
processed, 57
random, 21
related party, 40, 115
sales, 158–159
sampling, 69
search for, 21
sham, 42
suspicious, 16, 28, 36, 177,
    192–195
type, 31, 38, 56–57, 72
variations, 12–13, 59
Transactional:
    data, 22, 69
    fraud scheme variations, 59
    numbers, 72
    volume, 79
Travel expense schemes:
    airline ticket, 140
    altered, 141
    cash conversion, 142
    direct bill, 140
    disguised expenses, 141–142
    disguised trips, 141–142
    entertainment, 142
    multiple reimbursement, 140
    rental car, 143
    sex shop, 142

supervisor swap, 142
taxicab, 143
Trend analysis, 32

Understand factors, 29

Vendor(s):
    address, 24, 73–74, 93
    collude, 65
    database, 75
    different, 74–75, 140
    dormant, 86, 88, 93
    duties, 61
    false, 52
    favored, 26, 81, 121, 125, 130, 132
    fictitious, 44, 61, 75, 79, 86,
        112, 167
    fraudulent, 75
    identification, 43, 79–80, 86, 88,
        98, 126, 128, 130
    invoice, 15, 23–25, 30–31, 61,
        74, 79–80, 89–90, 92, 96, 98,
        148, 188
    master file, 30, 60–61, 74, 86, 104
    new, 61, 86, 88
    numbers, 75
    payment function, 30
    qualified, 130–132
    real, 75, 79, 93, 97–98, 102
    same, 104, 126, 134
    selected, 130
    temporary, 59, 86–88
Vendor schemes:
    bid rigging, 126, 132
    favored vendor, 26, 81, 121

Witnesses, 123, 165, 177–178,
    181,182

Lightning Source UK Ltd.
Milton Keynes UK
UKOW03n0110230414

230409UK00001B/11/P